CONTENTS

WORLD WAR I

Manfred von Richthofen	
William 'Billy' Bishop	8
Lawrence P. Coombes	10
Roderic S. Dallas	12
Carl Degelow	15
Werner Voss	18
Armand de Turenne	20
Edgar Taylor	23

WORLD WAR II

George Unwin	26
Helmut Wick	28
Nelville Duke	30
Peter Wykeham-Barnes	32
Donald McGee	34
Jack Storey	36
Clive Caldwell	38
Walter Nowotny	40
Pete Brothers	44
Günther Rall	46
Roy Whittaker	49
Lawrence 'Pinkie' Stark	52
Hiroyoshi Nishizawa	54
William 'Bill' Leverette	56
Hermann Graf	58
Eugeniusz Horbaczewski	61
Charles McCorckle	63
Willi Maximowitz	65
Clarence 'Bud' Anderson	68
Erich Hartmann	70
Heinz Bär	72
Sergei Dolgushin	74

POST-1945

James Jabara	76
Avihu Ben-Nun	78
Ra'anan Yosef	80

Copyright MyHobbyStore Ltd. 2011. All rights reserved

First published in Great Britain in 2010 by Osprey Publishing, Midland House, West Way, Botley, Oxford, OX2 0PH, UK
44-02 23rd Street, Suite 205A, Long Island City, NY 11101, USA

E-mail: info@ospreypublishing.com

Material for this booklet has been drawn exclusively from two previously published Osprey volumes: *Aircraft of the Aces: Legends of the Skies* and *Aircraft of the Aces: Legends of World War 2* compiled by Tony Holmes. All text and artwork is copyright to Osprey Publishing. Battlescene artwork is by Mark Postlethwaite and Iain Wyllie.

© 2011 Osprey Publishing Ltd.

All rights reserved. Apart from any fair dealing for the purpose of private study, research, criticism or review, as permitted under the Copyright, Designs and Patents Act, 1988, no part of this publication may be reproduced, stored in a retrieval system, or transmitted in any form or by any means, electronic, electrical, chemical, mechanical, optical, photocopying, recording or otherwise, without the prior written permission of the copyright owner. Inquiries should be addressed to the Publishers.
For a catalog of all books published by Osprey Publishing please contact:

NORTH AMERICA
Osprey Direct, c/o Random House Distribution Center,
400 Hahn Road, Westminster, MD 21157

Email: uscustomerservice@ospreypublishing.com

ALL OTHER REGIONS
Osprey Direct, The Book Service Ltd, Distribution Centre, Colchester Road, Frating Green, Colchester, Essex, CO7 7DW
E-mail: customerservice@ospreypublishing.com

Osprey Publishing is supporting the Woodland Trust, the UK's leading woodland conservation charity, by funding the dedication of trees.

www.ospreypublishing.com

INTRODUCTION

Rittmeister Manfred von Richthofen sits on a wheel of a Fokker triplane, which appears to be painted in factory finish – except perhaps for a red cowling? Note the manufacturer's plate on the cowling. Dogs were a favourite of many pilots, and here the Baron gazes at his Danish hound 'Moritz.'

Unsurprisingly, given their predilection for the dramatic hero, it was the French who first used the term 'ace' to describe successful aviators in the first year of World War 1. With trench warfare well and truly established by then, and hundreds of thousands of French troops being slaughtered in relative anonymity at the front, the national press looked to the skies to find a replacement for their heroes of the past – the cavalrymen. Instead of being saddled to a charger, the 'hussars' of the Great War were now strapped into an often equally temperamental fighting scout. Indeed, the frailty of these early aircraft was prematurely to end the career of the world's first ace, Roland Garros (he claimed six victories but only three of these were confirmed), when mechanical failure forced him down behind German lines on 19 April 1915.

By then, however, French journalists and publicists alike had already equated Garros's exploits with previous French military heroes. Fighting as an individual thousands of feet above the muddy trenches, his feats could be easily divorced from the mass destruction on the ground. These aerial battles received much coverage in the press, and quickly boosted flagging civilian morale on both sides of the front.

The first officially recognized ace was, appropriately, a French-man. Eugene Gilbert scored five victories in the spring of 1915 flying a two-seat Morane Type 'L' parasol monoplane. He was one of a handful of Allied pilots to gain, initially, the ascendancy over the Western Front, although this situation was soon reversed with the appearance of the legendary Fokker E-I Eindekker, flown by pilots of the caliber of Immelmann and Boelcke. These men were the first true fighter tacticians, revolutionizing air combat through the creation of a series of combat manoeuvres that are still employed by today's frontline fast jet pilots.

German aces dominated the skies, and the headlines, for much of World War 1, and today the world's most famous ace remains Rittmeister Freiherr Manfred von Richthofen, better known as the 'Red Baron'. Other notable aces from the conflict included 'Mick' Mannock, Billy Bishop, and Albert Ball of the Royal Flying Corps (RFC), Frenchmen Georges Guynemer, René Fonck, and Charles Nungesser, Americans Frank Luke and Eddie Rickenbacker, and German legends Ernst Udet, Werner Voss and Bruno Loerzer.

The myth of the ace was perpetuated during the 1920s and 30s through both factual and fictional accounts. Motivated by the feats of the aces of the Great War, and flying fighter aircraft that were far more effective in their designed role thanks to improvements in engine power, airframe design, and weaponry, pilots itched to get at the enemy. Many German and Japanese fighter pilots had a combat edge over their rivals in the early stages of the next world war due to their participation in earlier conflicts in Spain and China respectively. And a number of aces had been created during the fighting in both countries, pilots debuting the new generation of monoplane fighters such as the German Bf 109, Russian I-16, and Japanese Ki-97.

The German Blitzkrieg into Poland in September 1939, followed by the war in the west in May 1940, soon meant that Allied fighter pilots experienced the stark realities of modern aerial combat. In northern Europe, the Soviet invasion of Finland also resulted in a series of bitter aerial engagements, and war would continue to be waged between these two countries until 1944. Finally, the Italian declaration of war on Britain and France in June 1940 opened up new theatres for action over the deserts of North Africa and the warm waters of the Mediterranean.

Flying Nesher 10 from Refidim, Israeli ace Ra'anan Yosef was credited with his third, and last, kill on 19 October 1973, when he shot down this Egyptian MiG-21, whose brake-chute deployed possibly as a result of the damage inflicted by the burst of cannon fire from the Israeli jet. The starboard horizontal stabilizer also seems to have been badly damaged. Seconds later the Egyptian pilot ejected. *(via Shlomo Aloni)*

Just as in World War 1, the Germans coveted their aces, with the early exploits of men such as Mölders and Wick dominating the Nazi-controlled press. In Britain, the RAF once again played down the idea of aces, as it had done over two decades earlier. 'Better to favor the team than the individual' was the official policy, and the effects of this can still be seen today, with successful aces from World War 2 denigrating their role in the conflict for fear of being labelled 'line-shooters' by their contemporaries.

With the surprise German invasion of the USSR in June 1941 and the Japanese bombing of the US Pacific Fleet in Pearl Harbor six months later, World War 2 became a truly global conflict. The importance of air power, and the mastery of the skies, was understood by both sides, and the opportunities for men to make their mark in fighter aircraft abounded. Some German and Soviet aces, for example, racked up literally hundreds of kills over the Eastern Front.

The end of the war in 1945 brought a new era in combat aviation. With the advent of the jet fighter age and then indirect-fire air-to-air missiles (AAMs) from the 1950s and 60s, speed and technology became dominant in air warfare. Flying at two or three times the speed of the best World War 2 fighters, jet fighters such as the MiG-21 or Phantom F4 rarely experienced the time or space to engage in twisting dogfights. Furthermore, AAMs allied to radar later meant that targets could be engaged beyond visual range – now a pilot didn't even need to see his opponent to kill him. Combined with the often one-sided air superiority enforced by the superpowers, plus the greater investment in sophisticated surface-to-air anti-aircraft weaponry (a much cheaper prospect for many countries compared to jet fighters), and the kill tallies of World War 2 are now distant histories.

Yet even despite the surge of technology, the skills of the ace have remained relevant in the post-war world. In the skies over Korea, Vietnam and the Middle East, for example, fighter pilots still went head-to-head with enemy aircraft, sometimes with nothing more than cannon (often when missiles had been expended, or the range was too close). Even missile combat requires fighter pilots to know the rolls, flips and turns learnt by pilots during World War 1. More importantly, pilots require just as much courage and intelligence when taking their aircraft into hostile skies as they did nine decades ago. ∎

MANFRED VON RICHTHOFEN

The most successful fighter pilot of World War 1 was born on 2 May 1892 in the Lower Silesian town of Kleinberg, near Schweidnitz. An Army officer at the start of the war, he petitioned to transfer to the air service in May 1915. After a chance meeting with leading ace Oswald Boelcke, he was inspired to pursue pilot training, and completed this in December 1915. While serving as a pilot with Kampfgeschwader 2 in Russia, Richthofen was recruited for Boelcke's new Jasta 2. Flying the Albatros D II, he rewarded Boelcke's faith in him by downing an FE 2b on 17 September 1916 – the momentous first of an eventual 80 victories. After Boelcke's death on 28 October, Richthofen really showed his promise when he downed the DH 2 of Maj Lanoe G Hawker, the CO of No 24 Sqn and Britain's premier fighter tactician, on 23 November for his 11th victory.

On 10 January 1917, he was made commander of Jasta 11, and two days later received the news of his Pour le Mérite, which followed his 24th claim. Richthofen proved to be as skilful a leader, trainer and organizer as he was a fighter pilot. He rose to the rank of Rittmeister on 6 April. By the end of 'Bloody April' Richthofen had surpassed his idol Boelcke's score with 53 victories, and his Jasta 11 was famous throughout Germany. He was then given command of the first Fighter Wing in the Luftstreitkräfte, but his leadership of Jagdgeschwader Nr I was soon interrupted by a near-fatal head wound of 6 July. Richthofen returned to combat but was plagued by headaches and exhaustion. Nonetheless, his was a war of duty, and he persevered. In March and April 1918 he seemed to be back to his old form, scoring 16 kills in less than six weeks. His death on 21 April remains a subject of controversy, but his score would not be surpassed in World War 1, nor would his legend.

FOKKER DR I 425/17 OF RITTMEISTER MANFRED VON RICHTHOFEN, JG I, CAPPY, APRIL 1918

Richthofen's Dr I 425/17 (Wk-Nr 2009) was one of the few aircraft that the Rittmeister flew that was actually all-red – the smooth finish evident in photographs suggests it may have been painted this way at the factory. The Dr I is seen here in its final appearance, with narrow-chord cross bars and a white rudder.

AIRCRAFT SPECIFICATION
Fokker Dr I

TYPE:	single-seat, single-engined triplane fighter
ACCOMMODATION:	one pilot
DIMENSIONS:	length 18 ft 11 in (5.77 m) wingspan 23 ft 7.5 in (7.17 m) height 9 ft 8 in (2.95 m)
WEIGHTS:	empty 904 lb (410 kg) maximum take-off 1289 lb (585 kg)
PERFORMANCE:	maximum speed 103 mph (165 kmh) range, endurance of 1.5 hours powerplant Obursel Ur II output 110 hp (96.6 kW)
ARMAMENT:	two fixed Maxim LMG 08/15 7.92 mm machine guns immediately forward of the cockpit
FIRST FLIGHT DATE:	June 1917
OPERATOR:	Germany
PRODUCTION*:	320

Although aeronautical designers in Germany had been experimenting with triplane designs from aviation's earliest days, it was the appearance of the RNAS's Sopwith Triplane over the Western Front in late 1916 that prompted the hasty development of the Dr I. Created by Fokker's design team, the Dr I was a compact fighting scout that boasted wings without 'bracing' – it had no flying, landing or incidence wires, the airframe's strength instead coming from an original single-spar arrangement which was actually two boxspars joined vertically. Following successful type testing, the Dr I was ordered into production on 14 July 1917. The soundness of the design was proven the following month when two pre-production prototypes were tested at the front by Richthofen and fellow ace Werner Voss. An incredibly manoeuvrable aircraft about all axes, and very tiring to fly, the Dr I proved formidable with a skilled aviator at the controls, despite being rather slow and restricted to combat at lower altitudes. Briefly grounded in November 1917 due to a spate of wing failures caused by poor workmanship, the aircraft had all but disappeared at the front by August 1918. ∎

* number of aircraft built

WILLIAM 'BILLY' BARKER

William 'Billy' Barker was born in Canada in 1894. As a youth, he became an accomplished horseman and an excellent shot with a rifle. The eve of World War 1 found Barker living in Winnipeg, and in November 1914 he enlisted as as a private. By the time he arrived in France, via England, Barker had already applied to join the Royal Flying Corps (RFC). He saw brief action in the trenches prior to training as an observer and being posted to No 9 Sqn, which was equipped with BE 2s. Serving with similarly-equipped Nos 4 and 15 Sqns in France, Barker then retrained as a pilot and returned to No 15 Sqn in early 1917. While flying BE 2s, he won a Bar to the Military Cross (MC) that he had been awarded when serving as an observer.

Having tasted aerial combat, Barker asked for a transfer to single-seat fighters and was sent to No 28 Sqn, which was equipped with Camels. Soon becoming a flight commander, he scored three victories in France and then a further 19 in Italy following the unit's transfer to the Italian Front in November 1917. Barker then moved to No 66 Sqn, again as flight commander, and added 16 more victories to his tally, gaining a second Bar to his MC, plus a DSO and the Italian Silver Medal. Given command of No 139 Sqn, which flew Bristol F2b fighters, he took his Camel with him, and with it brought his score to 46, for which he was awarded a Bar to his DSO.

Later posted to France in a famous action on 27 October he was credited with four victories despite being heavily outnumbered. He was severely wounded in this dogfight, however, although it brought him the award of the Victoria Cross.

SNIPE E8102 OF MAJ 'BILLY' BARKER, ATTACHED TO NO 201 SQN, BEUGNÂTRE, OCTOBER 1918

This is the famous Snipe flown by Barker during his attachment to No 201 Sqn in France. His personal markings consisted of five thin white bands around the rear fuselage aft of the roundel, this decoration partially reflecting the markings he carried on the Camel that he flew in Italy. Another feature of his Italian Front Camel that was also present on the Snipe was a small, red, flat-metal devil thumbing his nose with both hands, which was affixed to the front of the starboard Vickers machine gun.

AIRCRAFT SPECIFICATION
Sopwith Snipe

TYPE:	single-seat, single-engined biplane fighter
ACCOMMODATION:	one pilot
DIMENSIONS:	length 19 ft 10 in (6.04 m) wingspan 31 ft 1 in (9.47 m) height 8 ft 3 in (2.51 m)
WEIGHTS:	empty 1312 lb (595 kg) maximum take-off 2020 lb (916 kg)
PERFORMANCE:	maximum speed 121 mph (195 kmh) range, endurance of 3 hours powerplant Bentley BR2 output 234 hp (172 kW)
ARMAMENT:	two fixed Vickers 0.303-in machine guns immediately forward of the cockpit
FIRST FLIGHT DATE:	September 1917
OPERATOR:	UK
PRODUCTION:	1100

Conceived as a replacement for the Camel, and designed from specifications given to Sopwith by the Air Board in early 1917, the Snipe looked every bit the big brother of the company's famed fighting scout. The specification called for a fighter that could attain 135 mph at 15,000 ft, sustain an average rate of climb of 1000 ft per minute above 10,000 ft and cruise at 25,000 ft. The aircraft also had to have an endurance of three hours. Once in service, the Snipe proved unable to reproduce any of these figures, despite being powered by the 230 hp Bentley BR2 engine. Ignoring these shortcomings, the RAF voiced its approval of the machine, and the Snipe was put into large-scale production. Of the 4500 ordered, 487 had been built by the end of December 1918, and production continued into the early 1920s. Examples started to arrive in France in August 1918, and No 43 Sqn was the first to swap its Camels for Snipes. The Australian Flying Corps' No 4 Sqn followed suit in October, and the final unit to receive examples prior to the Armistice was No 208 Sqn. Some 1100 Snipes were eventually built for the RAF, and the fighter remained in service until 1926. ∎

LAWRENCE P. COOMBES

Lawrence Percival Coombes was born in India on 9 April 1899, and he was just 19 when he joined the RNAS in June 1917. Upon completion of his pilot training he was posted to Teteghem-based 10 Naval Squadron in late January 1918. Coombes made his first claim just before his outfit became No 210 Sqn RAF, and by the end of July he had increased his score to 15 victories, and been awarded the DFC for his successes in combat.

In the spring of 1918, soon after the creation of the Royal Air Force on 1 April, Coombes and No 210 Sqn saw much action attacking enemy targets on the ground in an attempt to blunt the Germans' latest push in the bitterly contested Ypres sector. He enjoyed a lucky escape on 11 April when his Camel was badly shot up including the petrol tank.

One of the Camel ace's more memorable sorties occurred on 26 June when he and fellow aces Ivan Sanderson and American Ken Unger accounted for four Fokker D VIIs. One of the latter was flown by 13-kill Marine ace Kurt Schönfelder of Jasta 7, who had shot down Camel ace Pruett M Dennett of No 208 Sqn on 2 June (the German's last victory, claimed on 21 June, had also been a No 210 Sqn Camel). When not engaged in dogfighting, Coombes found himself readily employed in ground-attack sorties. Coombes managed to survive many such encounters, and post-war he became a barnstormer, before completing an engineering degree and eventually became chairman of the Commonwealth Advisory Aeronautical Research Council. Coombes passed away in Melbourne, Australia, on 2 June 1988.

CAMEL B6358 OF FLT SUB-LT LAWRENCE P COOMBES, 10 NAVAL SQUADRON, TREIZENNES, FRANCE, SPRING 1918

Coombes used B6358 to gain his first two victories. The aircraft had previously been on the strength of the Seaplane Defence Flight, where Flt Sub-Lt J E Greene had destroyed a balloon with it and had then endured a minor forced landing on 4 December 1917. Going to 9 Naval Squadron, the Camel had been used by Flt Sub-Lt M S Taylor to drive down a DFW in January, and after its spell with 10 Naval Squadron, B6358 went to No 213 Sqn. Here, Lt G D Smith shared a victory while flying the aircraft on 7 July. The veteran fighting scout was lost on 25 August 1918. While a part of 10 Naval Squadron, the Camel featured the unit's blue and white stripes, reaching back to the cockpit.

AIRCRAFT SPECIFICATION
Sopwith Camel

TYPE:	single-seat, single-engined biplane fighter
ACCOMMODATION:	one pilot
DIMENSIONS:	length 18 ft 9 in (5.72 m) wingspan 28 ft 0 in (8.53 m) height 8 ft 6 in (2.59 m)
WEIGHTS:	empty 929 lb (421 kg) maximum take-off 1453 lb (659 kg)
PERFORMANCE:	maximum speed 113 mph (182 kmh) range, endurance of 2.5 hours powerplant Clerget 9B, Bentley BR1 or Le Rhône output 130 hp (96.6 kW)
ARMAMENT:	two fixed Vickers 0.303-in machine guns immediately forward of the cockpit, and optional underwing racks for four 25 lb (11.3 kg) bombs
FIRST FLIGHT DATE:	22 December 1916
OPERATOR:	UK, USA
PRODUCTION:	5490

The most famous British fighter of World War 1, the Camel was also the most successful design to see service with either side in respect to the number of victories – 1294 aeroplanes and three airships – claimed by the men who flew it. Designed by Herbert Smith, the Camel was the first purpose-built fighting scout to boast two Vickers machine guns synchronized to fire through the propeller arc. The humped fairing covering the breeches of these weapons actually provided the inspiration for the fighter's unique sobriquet which, like its predecessor the Pup, went from being an unofficial appellation to its official name. Although the Camel boasted a fearsome reputation in combat, the fighter's exacting handling characteristics took a heavy toll on poorly trained novice pilots. Nevertheless, almost 5500 Camels were eventually built, with the Sopwith design seeing service on the Western Front with British (and American) units from May 1917 until war's end. ∎

On April 11 I was on another low bombing patrol.... I was flying at 300 ft when I was shot up from the ground. The engine stopped and I prepared to force-land when I felt petrol soaking the seat of my pants. I realised the main pressure tank on which the pilot sat was holed, so I switched to the gravity tank and the engine picked up. When I got back, it was found that besides the petrol tank, two cylinders had been pierced – it was a miracle the engine kept going.
– Lawrence P. Coombes

RODERIC S DALLAS

Born on 30 June 1891 in Mount Stanley, Queensland, Roderic Stanley Dallas joined the Australian Army in 1913 and received a commission several months later. Following the outbreak of World War 1 in August 1914, he applied for a transfer to the Royal Flying Corps (RFC) in the UK but was rejected. Unperturbed, Dallas then approached the Royal Navy, and was duly accepted by the Royal Naval Air Service (RNAS).

Commencing flying training in June 1915, he had his wings by November and joined 1 Naval Wing in Dunkirk on 3 December. Piloting two-seaters and single-seat Nieuport 11 Bébé scouts on reconnaissance patrols over the North Sea, often in terrible weather, Dallas' flying abilities rapidly developed to the point where he claimed his first three combat victories in April and May 1916 flying the diminutive French Bébé.

Sub-Lt Dallas officially achieved 'acedom' in the prototype Sopwith Triplane N500 on 9 July 1916 when he sent a Fokker E III down 'out of control' over Mariakerke. By February 1917 his score stood at seven, he had been awarded the Distinguished Service Cross and he was now a flight commander in the newly-established 1 Naval Squadron (formerly 1 Naval Wing). With the unit now fully equipped with Triplanes, it was sent to the Somme front in April to help hard-pressed RFC squadrons deal with the Fokker 'scourge'. Dallas made the most of this opportunity by claiming eight victories between 5 and 30 April, destroying two Albatros scouts on 22 April and recording the following his his logbook, 'Big scap – met the "Travelling Circus" – and Tom Culling, my valiant comrade in the air, went with me into a formation of 14 of them. We revved around and counter-attacked, so to speak, and in the general mix-up Culling got one and I got two.' Two more victories followed in May.

Given command of 'Naval 1' on 14 June, with his official score then standing at 17 victories, Dallas had boosted his tally to 23 by the time he left the unit in March 1918 – having flown Camels during his final eight months with 'Naval 1', Dallas became a SE 5a pilot when he was made CO of the RAF's No 40 Sqn in early April.

On 1 June 1918, with his overall score having reached 32 (some sources claim that it could be as high as 56), Dallas took off alone on a mid-morning patrol over the frontline. Flying west of the Allied trenches, he was attacked out of the clouds by a trio of Fokker Dr I triplanes from Jasta 14. Australia's second-ranking ace was fatally wounded when shots fired by Staffelführer Leutnant Johannes Werner hit the cockpit of his SE 5a, and he crashed to his death near Lievin – Dallas was Werner's sixth of seven victims.

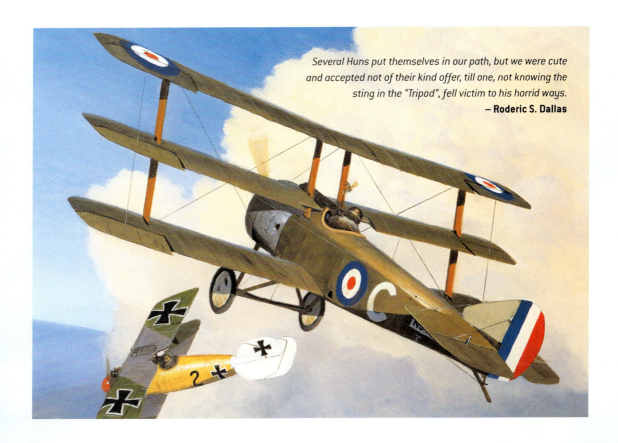

Several Huns put themselves in our path, but we were cute and accepted not of their kind offer, till one, not knowing the sting in the "Tripod", fell victim to his horrid ways.
— Roderic S. Dallas

TRIPLANE N5436 'C' OF SUB-LT RODERIC DALLAS, 1 NAVAL SQUADRON, LA BELLEVUE, FRANCE, APRIL 1917

Australian ace Roderic Stanley Dallas of 'Naval 1' flew this aircraft between December 1916 and May 1917, during which time he used it to claim 11 victories. Future ace C B Ridley then flew the veteran fighter in August and September 1917, scoring a further two victories with it. Very much a 'plain Jane' Triplane, it had a metal cowling and a clear-doped fin and wheel covers.

AIRCRAFT SPECIFICATION
Sopwith Triplane

TYPE:	single-seat, single-engined triplane fighter
ACCOMMODATION:	one pilot
DIMENSIONS:	length 18 ft 10 in (5.74 m) wingspan 26 ft 6 in (8.08 m) height 10 ft 6 in (3.20 m)
WEIGHTS:	empty 993 lb (450 kg) maximum take-off 1415 lb (642 kg)
PERFORMANCE:	maximum speed 116 mph (187 kmh) range, endurance of 2.75 hours powerplant Clerget 9B output 130 hp (96.6 kW)
ARMAMENT:	one (some with two) fixed Vickers 0.303-in machine gun immediately forward of the cockpit
FIRST FLIGHT DATE:	28 May 1916
OPERATOR:	UK, France
PRODUCTION:	150

Built as a replacement for the Pup, and boasting a fuselage similar to its famous forebear, the Triplane boasted a superior rate of climb and greatly improved manoeuvrability thanks to its extra wing. Indeed, when the type made its combat debut with the RNAS in late 1916, the Triplane could easily out-climb any other aircraft operated by either side over the Western Front. Aside from its use by the RNAS, the Triplane was also due to serve with the RFC, but a deal struck in February 1917 saw the Navy exchange all its SPAD VIIs for all the Triplanes then on order for the RFC. This agreement subsequently resulted in the planned production run for the Triplane being rapidly scaled back, and only 150 were completed. Nevertheless, the design had a great impact when it finally met the enemy – so much so that the German High Command immediately ordered their manufacturers to produce triplane designs to counter the Sopwith fighter, the most famous of which was the Fokker Dr I. Aside from the Triplane's use by the RNAS, 16 examples were also supplied to the French Navy in mid 1917. Naval squadrons on the Western Front began replacing their well used Triplanes with Camels from July 1917 onwards, and the last examples in frontline service were flown by Home Defence units in southern England. ■

CARL DEGELOW

Carl Degelow was born in January 1891 in Müsterdorf. Pre-war, he had worked in the USA as an industrial chemist, and therefore spoke English well. Degelow returned to Germany shortly before the outbreak of war to enlist in the second Nassauischen Infanterie-Regiment Nr 88, seeing action in France and Russia. Commissioned in July 1915, he transferred to the aviation service the following year, and was sent to Fl. Abt. (A) 216 on the Somme at the beginning of 1917. Degelow's aggressive flying got him moved to fighters, and Jasta 7, and by mid-May 1918 he had scored a handful of victories prior to his transfer to Jasta 40. After the death, on 9 July, of previous leader Helmuth Dilthey, Degelow took over the unit.

He picked up his first Fokker D VII on 25 June 1918. After having Staffel mechanics check it over and load the ammunition, Degelow took it up for a brief hop. During this 'test flight' he encountered a scrap between Camels and D VIIs of another Jasta, and duly downed a Sopwith attacking one of the Fokkers – it was his sixth victory. Degelow's claims from July onwards were attained with the D VII, six aircraft falling to his guns in that first month. He was on leave in August, but added six more victories in September, ten in October and one – his 30th and last – on 4 November.

Degelow survived the war to write a short memoir, *Mit dem weissen Hirsch durch dick und dünn* (*With the White Stag through Thick and Thin*). In 1979, nine years after Degelow's death, historian Peter Kilduff expanded on this work, using extensive interviews and additional material to produce *Germany's Last Knight of the Air*, which provides an excellent view of 4th Army D VII operations.

His memoir graphically recalls what it was like to participate in a dogfight in the skies above the Western Front. In particular, he recalled a dramatic struggle on 24 September 1918 when he led his pilots against ten Whitworth FK 8 bombers and their escorts of SE 5a fighters:

> We gained altitude and caught the British SE 5s from the least expected point – right beneath their floorboards. I closed in on a fellow with a big white 'Y' painted on his top wing… Nothing I did could entice him to come down to my level. So, after we wildly stormed round and round each other a few times, I tried to bluff him. I pulled my Fokker straight up, and for one advantageous moment I had the SE 5 squarely in front of my guns. I pressed the buttons of my machine guns, really only to intimidate my partner by the fire, and hopefully to get him to give up his advantageous altitude and dive for the ground. But, in so doing, some of my shots, which were surely accidental hits, went into the reserve fuel tank of the enemy aircraft.
>
> Bright flames immediately burst from the emergency fuel supply on the top wing, where it was located on the SE. I was very pleased by my bluff, and believed the enemy now to be finished.

Then, with his machine glowing with fire, he dived right at me, all the while maintaining a murderous stream of fire from his machine guns.
— **Carl Degelow**

FOKKER D VII (ALB) OF LTN D R CARL DEGELOW, JASTA 40, LOMME, AUGUST 1918

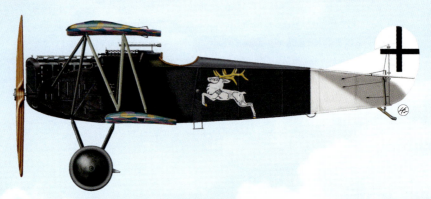

Jasta 40's D VIIs all sported black fuselages, augmented by a white tail unit. Cabane and landing gear struts and wheel covers were also black. The wings of this Albatros-built D VII are covered in five-colour fabric, with blue rib tapes and a diagonal white stripe on the top wing to identify the Staffelführer. Degelow's 'white stag' emblem displays golden yellow antlers and hooves.

AIRCRAFT SPECIFICATION
Fokker D VII

TYPE:	single-seat, single-engined biplane fighter
ACCOMMODATION:	one pilot
DIMENSIONS:	length 22 ft 9.66 in (6.95 m) wingspan 29 ft 2.333 in (8.90 m) height 9 ft 0 in (2.75 m)
WEIGHTS:	empty 1508 lb (684 kg) maximum take-off 2006 lb (910 kg)
PERFORMANCE:	maximum speed 116 mph (187 kmh) range, endurance of 1.5 hours powerplant Mercedes D IIIaü output 180 hp (134 kW)
ARMAMENT:	two fixed Maxim LMG 08/15 7.92 mm machine guns immediately forward of the cockpit
FIRST FLIGHT DATE:	December 1917
OPERATOR:	Germany
PRODUCTION:	2000+

The arrival of the Fokker D VII at the front in late April 1918 finally began to redress the balance in favour of the German Air Service, whose pilots had had to fly obsolete Albatros D V, D Va and Pfalz D IIIs against superior Allied types such as the SE 5a, Sopwith Triplane and Camel, Bristol F 2B, the French SPAD VII and later SPAD XIII. The battle for air supremacy over the trenches was paramount to both sides so that their armies could launch assaults with support from the air. Fokker's Dr I had briefly redressed the balance in late 1917, yet even Manfred von Richthofen was fully aware that the life of the triplane was limited, and a new machine was desperately needed. He was among the aces who had tested the new Fokker biplane prototype, and was eager to see its arrival at the front. Indeed, one of the last things he did prior to his death in action on 21 April 1918 was write to the German Air Service High Command seeking news on the availability of the D VII. 'After a long time I come once again with a question. When can I count on the arrival of Fokker biplanes with the super-compressed engines? The superiority of British single-seat and reconnaissance aircraft makes it even more perceptibly unpleasant here. The single-seaters fight coming over at high altitude and stay there. One cannot even shoot at them. Speed is the most important point. One could shoot down five to ten times as many if we were faster. Please give me news soon about when we can count on these new machines.' ∎

WERNER VOSS

Werner Voss was born in Krefeld on 13 April 1897. When he was 17, he enlisted in his local militia, then went to war with the 2. Westfälische Husaren Regiment Nr 11 – a unit known as the 'dancing hussars'. Like so many other cavalrymen, the stalemate of trench warfare failed to meet his expectations, and he transferred into aviation in August 1915. Once trained, Voss was assigned to Kasta 20 of Kagohl IV, and he began his career as a pilot in the Verdun area. He was happily transferred to Jasta Boelcke on 21 November 1916, and opened his account with two victories six days later.

Voss scored rapidly in early 1917 and with his tally at 24, he received the 'Blue Max' on 8 April. This was followed by routine leave, during which Voss missed most of the killing time of 'Bloody April'. Voss was given acting command of Jasta 5 on 20 May, then a scant nine days later he moved to Jasta 29. His time as Staffelführer only lasted five days, whereupon he went to command Jasta 14. At the end of July 1917 his old comrade Manfred von Richthofen called upon him to take command of Jasta 10, and Voss was soon building up the score of this previously lackluster unit. Issued with one of the first Fokker F I triplanes to reach the front in early September 1917, Voss saw considerable action in the machine up until his death in action in a much storied clash with seven SE 5as of the crack No 56 Sqn on 23 September 1917. Aged just 20, Voss had been credited with 48 victories prior to his death.

ALBATROS D III OF LEUTNANT WERNER VOSS, JASTA 2 BOELCKE AND JASTA 5, MID 1917

Werner Voss, during his period with Jasta Boelcke, flew this much-decorated Albatros D III. When interviewed by historian Alex Imrie (circa 1960), Voss's motor mechanic Karl Timm recalled that the ace instructed him and Flieger Christian Rüser (the airframe mechanic) to paint a red heart with white border on both sides of the fuselage. Then Voss had them add a white swastika (merely a good luck symbol at this time). Timm told Voss he thought this looked a bit bare, and suggested that he add a laurel wreath around the swastika, which the pilot agreed to. Voss continued to fly this D III in these markings at Jasta 5, but it almost certainly did not follow him to Jasta 10.

AIRCRAFT SPECIFICATION
Albatros D III

TYPE:	single-seat, single-engined biplane fighter
ACCOMMODATION:	one pilot
DIMENSIONS:	length 24 ft 0 in (7.33 m) wingspan 29 ft 8 in (9.04 m) height 9 ft 9.25 in (2.98 m)
WEIGHTS:	empty 1457 lb (661 kg) maximum take-off 1953 lb (886 kg)
PERFORMANCE:	maximum speed 107 mph (180 kmh) range 217 miles (350 km) powerplant Mercedes D III output 160 hp (119.2 kW)
ARMAMENT:	two fixed Maxim LMG 08/15 7.92 mm machine guns immediately forward of the cockpit
FIRST FLIGHT DATE:	August 1916
OPERATOR:	Germany, Austria-Hungary, Turkey
PRODUCTION:	1532

Designed to wrest from the Allies the aerial superiority gained by the Nieuport 11 Bébé and Airco DH 2 over the once all-conquering Fokker E III, the Albatros-Werke machines made their combat debut in the summer of 1916. The first of the genus, the D I and D II had an immediate impact on the air war in the fall of that year, these fighters establishing new standards in airframe elegance. Boasting a neatly cowled Mercedes D III inline engine and a carefully streamlined semi-monocoque wooden fuselage, the Albatros scout looked like nothing else at the front at that time. They were also the first quantity-produced fighters to mount twin-synchronized machine guns. The D III was a further evolution of the Albatros D I/II design, this version abandoning the solid parallel-structure single-bay wing cellule in favor of the lighter, lower-drag Nieuport-style sesquiplane cellule. Some 400 were ordered by the Germans in October 1916, and production examples reached frontline Jastas from December of that same year. Early D IIIs suffered from chronic wing failure in the first months of operational service due to torsional flexibility of the lower wing – reinforced wings were introduced with the second batch of 840 machines. The D III was also licence-built by Oeffag in Austria, and these were progressively fitted with more powerful engines that produced up to 225 hp. Some 220 examples were also supplied to the Austro-Hungarians in 1917–18, and Poland procured 60 Oeffag-built machines post-war. The D III disappeared from service over the Western Front during mid 1918, but saw combat with the Austro-Hungarians until war's end. ■

ARMAND DE TURENNE

Armand Jean Galliot Joseph de Turenne was born on 1 April 1891 in Le Mans, the son of a former infantry officer. Upon his graduation from school, he enlisted for three years military duty with 10éme Regiment de Chasseurs in April 1909. Following a brief return to civilian life, Turenne re-enlisted in the 21ére Regiment de Dragoons in February 1913. Promoted to officer candidate in August of the following year, he requested a transfer to the aviation service in July 1915 and received his brevet as a pilot on 21 December that same year following the completion of his training at Pau.

Turenne was posted to Nieuport-equipped Escadrille N48 (led by Lt Georges Matton) on 14 June 1916, and after seeing much action over the Verdun front, he scored his first victory on 17 November when he downed an Albatros. On 6 July 1917, he was patrolling alongside his CO near Reims when they encountered six Albatros D Vs just over the French side of the frontline. Turenne later recalled how the dogfight unfolded:

> Eager to show my squadron leader, I rushed onto them, took a shot at them and missed. Immediately, I had two of them on my tail and was in a very bad spot. Matton chased one of the Germans and shot him down, then the others fled towards the German lines. I managed to chase one and catch up with him. He was going down, weaving to avoid my bursts of fire, but I got his engine and he had to make an emergency landing in our lines. I circled over him because I could see his propeller still turning. Then I saw the pilot jump out of the machine and lay on the ground while the aeroplane rolled along and crashed into a fence 50 yards ahead. The German had sabotaged his machine according to orders.

By the end of September 1917 he had increased his tally to six victories (all fighting scouts), and his leadership qualities were recognised on 12 January the following year when he was made CO of Escadrille SPA12. Under Turenne's leadership, the unit was cited in General Orders on 14 May 1918 for having downed 34 aircraft and two balloons.

Promoted to capitaine in July 1918, Turenne claimed his last two victories on 26 September in an action which almost cost him his life. Wounded twice already during the course of the year while attacking observation balloons, he destroyed another near Verdun for his 14th victory, but was then set upon by several Fokker D VIIs. Turenne's SPAD XIII was badly shot up and the Frenchman slightly wounded, but by playing dead he managed to lure one of his attackers into an advantageous position and shoot him down for his final victory. During the final month of the war Turenne was placed in command of Groupe de Combat 11.

Remaining in military service post-war, Turenne had made full colonel by March 1937. He again fought for his country in 1939–40 as commander of Groupe de Chasse 24, and was promoted to a Grand Officier de la Legion d'Honneur on 25 December 1941. Turenne finally passed away in December 1980.

I managed to chase one and catch up with him. He was going down, weaving to avoid my bursts of fire, but I got his engine and he had to make an emergency landing in our lines.
— **Armand de Turenne**

SPAD VII (SERIAL UNKNOWN) OF LT ARMAND DE TURENNE, SPA48, JULY 1917

Turenne claimed that he and his commander, Lt Georges Matton, co-designed the cockerel's head within a blue halo that was ultimately adopted as N48's squadron insignia, along with the motto Chant et Combat ('Crow and Fight'). In addition to the cockerel insignia and the number '2', Turenne retained the family coat of arms that had graced the side of his earlier Nieuport 11, applied under the cockpit of his SPAD VII. Later, when he took command of SPA12 in 1918, Turenne retained the SPA 48 cockerel's head as a personal marking in place of SPA12's usual blue and white pennant, but dispensed with an individual numeral, since his marking was unique within the escadrille.

AIRCRAFT SPECIFICATION
SPAD VII

TYPE:	single-seat, single-engined biplane fighter
ACCOMMODATION:	one pilot
DIMENSIONS:	length 19 ft 11.3 in (6.08 m) wingspan 25 ft 8 in (7.82 m) height 7 ft 2.75 in (2.20 m)
WEIGHTS:	empty 1102 lb (500 kg) maximum take-off 1552 lb (704 kg)
PERFORMANCE:	maximum speed 132 mph (212 kmh) range, endurance of 1.85 hours powerplant Hispano-Suiza HS 8Ab output 180 hp (134 kW)
ARMAMENT:	one fixed Vickers 7.7 mm machine gun immediately forward of the cockpit
FIRST FLIGHT DATE:	April 1916
OPERATOR:	France, UK, USA, Russia, Belgium, Italy
PRODUCTION:	5500

The end result of the design trend of 1915–16 which saw heavier, more powerful and less agile fighting scouts appearing from the warring nations of Europe, the SPAD VII was easily the most successful aircraft of this period to emerge from France. Powered by the superb, but often temperamental, Hispano-Suiza V8 engine, the 150 hp SPAD VII prototype had flown for the first time in April 1917. The aircraft had an impressive top speed in both level flight and in the dive, but lacked the manoeuvrability of contemporary Nieuports. However, combat reports received from the front had suggested that pilots valued high speed over agility, hence the heavy fighter route chosen by SPAD. Production examples began reaching French combat units in the summer of 1916, but the delivery tempo was slow due to production difficulties with the scout's V8 engine. The SPAD VII entered combat with both the French Aviation Militaire and the RFC at much the same time, and once its engine maladies had been rectified, the fighter enjoyed great success over the Western Front. Most French escadrille de chasse flew the SPAD VII at some stage in World War 1, and the aircraft also saw action with Belgian, Italian, American and Russian units during the conflict. ■

EDGAR TAYLOR

One of a number of American citizens to see action with the RFC/RAF and RNAS rather than the US Air Service, despite the US declaration of war with Germany in 1917, Edgar Taylor of Central Falls, Rhode Island, joined the RFC in early 1918. After earning his wings, he was posted to No 79 Sqn at Beauvois in April. The unit had been assigned to frontline flying just a matter of weeks before, equipped with the then new Sopwith Dolphin.

After a slow start, Taylor gained his first victory on 4 August, when he destroyed a Fokker D VII. Taylor then took on the challenge of balloon-busting, destroying four of these dangerous targets during the same month. Captive or kite balloons, also known as *Drachens* and 'Sausages', were the oldest form of aerial reconnaissance, first being used by the French in 1795. They saw considerable use during World War 1, since they could stay in the air longer than aeroplanes and, thanks to their stabilising fins, they provided the observer with a steady platform from which to scan a large proportion of the frontline. Communicating by telephone with forces on the ground, the balloon observers could direct artillery fire or detect frontline movements, and as such, they constituted a very real menace to the other side's troops. Destroying enemy balloons, therefore, was a very desirable objective before a major offensive, defensive or logistics support was to be carried out.

Most airmen regarded balloon-busting missions as extraordinarily difficult and dangerous. The balloons were located deep within enemy lines, requiring their attackers to go after them, exposed to observation, fighters and every enemy soldier carrying a gun.

Each balloon was surrounded by a corden of anti-aircraft guns and even if pilots reached the balloon it was surprisingly difficult to ignite pure hydrogen, even with incendiary bullets. While once lit the burning balloon could be seen for miles ensuring that any likely escape route would be rapidly blocked by converging enemy fighters. As a result, balloon-busting was regarded as a suicide-mission, requiring as much luck as skill on the pilot's part, and an aeroplane capable of standing up to considerable punishment.

Edgar Taylor was hit by ground fire in the process of claiming his last balloon victim on the 24th, and was mortally wounded. He was just 20 and has no known grave.

Once ignited, a burning balloon could be seen for miles, assuring confirmation for the fighter pilot who destroyed it – provided he returned to claim the kill.
— Edgar Taylor

DOLPHIN D3727 OF LT EDGAR TAYLOR, NO 79 SQN, STE-MARIE-CAPPEL, AUGUST 1918

American Lt Edgar Taylor gained all five of his victories with D3727, and he was also mortally wounded at its controls. Marked with the identification letter 'J' aft of the unit's white square marking, which was repeated on the top port wing inboard of the roundel, this aircraft served with No 79 Sqn from 16 June to 24 August 1918, when it was lost in action. D3727 had completed 97 flying hours prior to its final sortie.

AIRCRAFT SPECIFICATION

Sopwith Dolphin

TYPE:	single-seat, single-engined biplane fighter
ACCOMMODATION:	one pilot
DIMENSIONS:	length 22 ft 3 in (6.78 m) wingspan 32 ft 6 in (9.90 m) height 8 ft 6 in (2.59 m)
WEIGHTS:	empty 1466 lb (665 kg) maximum take-off 2000 lb (907 kg)
PERFORMANCE:	maximum speed 128 mph (206 kmh) range 195 miles (315 km) powerplant Hispano-Suiza 8E output 200 hp (149 kW)
ARMAMENT:	two fixed Vickers 0.303-in machine guns immediately forward of the cockpit and one or two moveable Lewis 0.303-in machine guns mounted over the top wing
FIRST FLIGHT DATE:	May 1917
OPERATOR:	UK
PRODUCTION:	1532

Built as a Camel replacement, the Dolphin was unique in that it was the first multi-gun fighter to see action during World War 1. It was also the first active Sopwith machine not to be fitted with a rotary engine. The Dolphin was designed with two belt-fed 0.303-in Vickers guns mounted in front of the windscreen in the pilot's line of sight, and it was also capable of having two drum-fed 0.303-in Lewis guns fixed to the cockpit cross-member connecting the two upper wings. When Sopwith's chief designer Herbert Smith was tasked with creating the Dolphin in the spring of 1917, he determined to produce a machine that gave its pilot the best possible all-round visibility. He achieved this by putting the pilot's eye-line above the upper wings. To further improve visibility downwards, he removed the centre section from the upper wings and back-staggered them by 13 inches in comparison with the lower wings. As he had done with the Camel, Smith designed his new machine with all its mass – engine, guns, petrol tank and pilot – grouped together 'up front', so that the Dolphin would inherit the high degree of manoeuvrability associated with his previous Sopwith fighting scout. The first production examples reached No 19 Sqn in the final week of 1917, and by 9 January 1918 the unit had exchanged all of its SPAD VIIs for Dolphins. The aircraft flew its first combat patrol on 3 February, and by month-end the Dolphin had claimed its first victories. ∎

GEORGE UNWIN

After a long chase, I finally caught them as they crossed the Kent coast at Lydd, and after firing a long burst into the trailing fighter, it immediately burst into flames and crashed just offshore. – George Unwin

A member of No 19 Sqn from 1936, and one of the RAF's most experienced Spitfire service pilots at the outbreak of war, Flt Sgt George 'Grumpy' Unwin was the unit's senior NCO throughout the long summer of 1940. First engaging the enemy over the evacuation beaches of Dunkirk during Operation *Dynamo*, he was later awarded the Distinguished Flying Medal (DFM) and Bar for his successful participation in both this action and the Battle of Britain. By the time he was posted away from the unit at the end of 1940, having been deemed too old at 28 by Fighter Command to serve within its frontline force, Unwin had been credited with 13 and 2 shared aircraft confirmed destroyed, two unconfirmed victories and a solitary damaged claim. These successes made him No 19 Sqn's leading ace of 1940.

Unwin later recalled why he enjoyed success in the Spitfire during that fateful year: 'We were always on the defensive during 1940 due to the ceiling advantage enjoyed by the enemy. Our staple tactic to counter this was to turn straight into them so that they couldn't latch onto your tail. You then pulled on the "g" in the hope that your own superior rate of turn would allow you to whip around on their tails.'

In old age, George 'Grumpy' Unwin lived quietly in Dorset, his modest abode backing onto a golf course on which he played a round virtually every day. His RAF career spanned three decades across the globe, and he eventually attained the rank of wing commander. However, he categorically stated that his two-and-a-half year spell as an NCO on Spitfires (during which time he flew no less than 48 different aircraft) with No 19 Sqn at Duxford was the pinnacle of his career as a fighter pilot. Unwin died in June 2006.

SPITFIRE MK IB R6776/'QV-H' OF FLT SGT GEORGE UNWIN, NO 19 SQN, FOWLMERE, AUGUST/ SEPTEMBER 1940

This aircraft was one of the original cannon-armed Spitfire IBs issued to No 19 Sqn for a brief period in the summer of 1940. Unlike the majority of the unit's pilots, who struggled with the reliability of the twin cannon armament in their Mk IBs, Unwin enjoyed some success in this aircraft, claiming a Bf 110 destroyed and another probably destroyed on 16 August, followed by a third Bf 110 confirmed destroyed on 3 September. Later, the aircraft was modified into a Mk VB, and went on to serve with Nos 92, 316 and 306 Sqns, before being written off in May 1942.

AIRCRAFT SPECIFICATION
Supermarine Spitfire Mk I/II
(all dimensions and performance data for Spitfire Mk IA)

TYPE:	single-engined monoplane fighter
ACCOMMODATION:	one pilot
DIMENSIONS:	length 29 ft 11 in (9.12 m) wingspan 36 ft 10 in (11.23 m) height 11 ft 5 in (3.48 m)
WEIGHTS:	empty 4810 lb (2182 kg) loaded weight 5844 lb (2651 kg)
PERFORMANCE:	maximum speed 355 mph (571 kmh) range 575 miles (925 km) powerplant Rolls-Royce Merlin II/III output 1030 hp (768 kW)
ARMAMENT:	eight 0.303 in machine guns in wings
FIRST FLIGHT DATE:	5 March 1936
OPERATOR:	Australia, Canada, New Zealand, UK
PRODUCTION:	1567 Mk Is and 921 Mk IIs

The only British fighter to remain in production throughout World War 2, the exploits of the Supermarine Spitfire are legendary. More than 20,000 were produced in mark numbers ranging from I through to 24, this total also including over 1000 built as dedicated Seafire fleet fighters for the Royal Navy. Designed by Reginald J Mitchell following his experiences with the RAF's Schneider Trophy winning Supermarine floatplanes of the 1920s and 30s, prototype Spitfire K5054 first took to the skies on 6 March 1936, powered by the soon to be equally famous Rolls-Royce Merlin I engine. However, due to production problems encountered with the revolutionary stressed-skin construction of the fighter, it was to be another two-and-a-half years before the first examples entered service with Fighter Command. Spitfire Mk Is and IIs served only briefly in frontline squadrons with the RAF (exclusively on the Channel Front) once the war had started, but their pilots were responsible for achieving impressive scores against the all-conquering Luftwaffe during the Battles of France and Britain. Although early-mark Spitfires were notorious for their light armament, overheating engines due to inadequate cooling and short range, many of the pilots that flew the Mk Is and IIs regarded the first production machines as the best handling of the breed, being a 'true aviator's aircraft' due to its excellent power-to-weight ratio and beautifully harmonized flying controls. ∎

HELMUT WICK

The meteoric rise of Helmut Wick – from a Rottenführer (leader of a two-aircraft formation) to Geschwaderkommodore of JG 2 'Richthofen', the Luftwaffe's premier fighter unit – was unparalleled in the annals of that service's history.

As a 24-year-old Leutnant, it was Wick who scored JG 2's first victory of World War 2 when he downed a French Curtiss Hawk on 22 November 1939. He did not add to his own tally until the Blitzkrieg was well underway, claiming a trio of LeO 451 bombers on 17 May 1940. But in the six months which followed, a steady succession of victories would make Wick the most successful fighter pilot of the entire Luftwaffe.

He emerged from the Battle of France with 14 kills and in July 1940 he was appointed Staffelkapitän of 3./JG 2. It was during the Battle of Britain that his dual qualities of marksmanship and leadership really came to the fore. A lengthening list of successes earned Wick awards, promotion, and the adulation of the German press, and on 27 August, as an Oberleutnant, he received the Knight's Cross for 20 victories. He became Gruppenkommandeur of I./JG 2 the following month, and was awarded the Oak Leaves on 6 October – by which time his score had risen to 42.

Already a major, Wick was given command of JG 2 'Richthofen' exactly a fortnight later. But fate was soon to overtake him in the skies south of the Isle of White, during an action against No 609 Sqn with Flt Lt John Dundas and Sgt Zygmunt Klein. The solitary parachute drifting down towards the sea was the last anyone saw of Wick. Confirmation of who shot him down remains as mystery as both the British pilots were also lost.

BF 109E-4 (WK-NR 5344) 'BLACK DOUBLE CHEVRON' OF HAUPTMANN HELMUT WICK, GRUPPENKOMMANDEUR OF I./JG 2 'RICHTHOFEN', BEAUMONT-LE-ROGER, OCTOBER 1940

Depicted midway in its evolution from 'Yellow 2' to full Kommodore's markings, Wk-Nr 5344 is shown in profile soon after it had received its coat of very close dapple overall. Note also the 'toning down' of the fuselage cross by reducing the white areas, and the pale yellow cowling (thin yellow wash over white). Certain inconsistencies in the presentation and grouping of the victory bars point to 5344's having had a number of replacement rudders during its career. The 'Richthofen' Geschwader badge is carried beneath the windscreen, while that on the cowling (long thought to be Wick's personal emblem) is the insignia of 3./JG 2, designed some time earlier by a Staffel member who chose the colors blue and yellow in honor of the then Kapitän Hennig Strümpell's Swedish ancestry.

AIRCRAFT SPECIFICATION
Messerschmitt Bf 109E
(all dimensions and performance data for Bf 109E-3)

TYPE:	single-engined monoplane fighter
ACCOMMODATION:	one pilot
DIMENSIONS:	length 28 ft 0 in (8.55 m) wingspan 32 ft 4.5 in (9.87 m) height 8 ft 2 in (2.49 m)
WEIGHTS:	empty 4189 lb (1900 kg) maximum take-off 5875 lb (2665 kg)
PERFORMANCE:	maximum speed 348 mph (560 kmh) range 410 miles (660 km) powerplant Daimler-Benz DB 601Aa output 1175 hp (876 kW)
ARMAMENT:	two 7.9 mm machine guns in upper cowling, two 20 mm cannon in wings; some E-3s had additional 20 mm cannon in propeller hub; fighter-bomber (250-kg) bomb under fuselage
FIRST FLIGHT DATE:	June 1937 (Bf 109 V10)
OPERATOR:	Bulgaria, Croatia, Germany, Romania, Slovakia, Spain, Switzerland, Yugoslavia
PRODUCTION:	approximately 4000

Designed to meet a 1934 Reichluftfahrtministerium (RLM) requirement for a single-seat monoplane fighter, the original Bf 109 V1 was the winning competitor in a 'fly off' that involved three other designs from proven German aviation companies. Light and small, the first production-standard Bf 109s (B-1 models) to enter service in early 1937 proved their worth during the Spanish Civil War. By the time Germany invaded Poland in September 1939, the re-engined Bf 109E was rolling off the Messerschmitt production line in great quantity, the now-familiar airframe being paired up with the powerful Daimler-Benz DB 601. This combination had been tested as long ago as June 1937, when a pre-production aircraft had been flown with a carburetted DB 600 fitted in place of the D-model's Junkers Jumo 210Da, but the subsequent availability of the Bf 109E had been hampered by delays in the development of the appreciably more powerful Daimler-Benz engine. However, these problems had been sorted out by early 1939. Built in huge numbers, and in a great array of sub-variants for the fighter, reconnaissance, fighter-bomber and shipboard fighter roles, the Bf 109E proved to be the master of all its European contemporaries bar the Spitfire Mk I/II, to which it was considered an equal. Aside from fighting over Poland, the E-model saw combat throughout the Blitzkrieg of 1940 and the Battle of Britain which followed, in the Balkans in 1941 and in the opening phases of the North African and Soviet campaigns. ∎

NEVILLE DUKE

Born in Tonbridge, Kent, Neville Duke joined the RAF in 1940, and in April of the following year was posted to No 92 Sqn at Biggin Hill. By the end of August he had claimed two enemy aircraft destroyed and a further two damaged (all Bf 109Fs), and he was quickly picked out as a talented novice.

In November 1941 Duke was posted to No 112 Sqn in North Africa, and flying firstly the Tomahawk and then the Kittyhawk, he rapidly built up his score. Having completed his first tour by February 1942, he served as an instructor at the fighter School at El Ballah, in Egypt, before returning to No 92 Sqn as a flight commander in November of that same year. Operating Spitfire VB Trops, the unit saw much action during the invasion of Tunisia, and Duke continued to claim victories. Following the end of his second tour in June 1943, he was then promoted to squadron leader, and spent a further period at a training unit at Abu Sueir, again in Egypt, as its Chief Flying Instructor. In March 1944 he assumed command of No 145 Sqn, flying Spitfire VIIIs, in Italy, and by September Duke had become the top scoring RAF fighter pilot in the Mediterranean theatre.

He returned to the United Kingdom in October 1944 and was allocated to Hawker Aircraft Ltd as a production test pilot. Post-war he joined the RAF High Speed Flight in June 1946. In 1948 he left the service and returned to Hawker to work as a test pilot. Whilst at Hawker he carried out much of the early test flying of the company's successful Hunter jet fighter, setting a new world speed record in 1953.

SPITFIRE MK VB TROP ER220/'QJ-R' OF FLG OFF NEVILLE DUKE, NO 92 SQN, WADDI SURRI, LIBYA, LATE JANUARY 1943

Delivered to No 9 Maintenance Unit (MU) at RAF Cosford on the last day of August 1942, this aircraft was subsequently passed on to No 47 MU at Sealand two weeks later. Here, it was prepared for shipping to North Africa, and then loaded aboard the vessel *Empire Liberty* along with a number of other Mk VB Trops. The aircraft departed British shores on 19 September, and according to its record card, was next noted at No 116 MU's aircraft assembly facility at Takoradi, on the Gold Coast, on 7 November. ER220 was issued to No 92 Sqn as an attrition replacement in November 1942, and its arrival coincided with Neville Duke's posting to the unit after a six-month spell 'resting'. He would go on to score two kills in the aircraft, his first claim being against a C.202 that he downed near Zidan, in Tunisia, on 8 January. He followed this with the Ju 87 victory. ER220 was passed on to No 601 Sqn soon afterwards, and was shot down by a Bf 110 from III./ZG 26 off Cap Bon, on the Tunisian coast, on 17 April 1943. Its pilot, Flt Sgt P F Griffiths, bailed out over the sea and was subsequently captured.

AIRCRAFT SPECIFICATION
Supermarine Spitfire Mk V
(all dimensions and performance data for Spitfire Mk VB/C)

TYPE:	single-engined monoplane fighter
ACCOMMODATION:	one pilot
DIMENSIONS:	length 29 ft 11 in (9.12 m) wingspan 36 ft 10 in (11.23 m) height 11 ft 5 in (3.48 m)
WEIGHTS:	empty 5100 lb (2313 kg) loaded weight 6785 lb (3078 kg)
PERFORMANCE:	maximum speed 374 mph (602 kmh) range 470 miles (756 km) powerplant Rolls-Royce Merlin 45/50/55/56 output 1470 hp (1096 kW)
ARMAMENT:	four 0.303 in machine guns and two 20 mm cannon in wings (VC had provision for two or four 20 mm cannon in wings); provision for one 500-lb (227-kg) or two 250-lb (113-kg) bombs externally
FIRST FLIGHT DATE:	December 1940
OPERATOR:	Australia, Canada, Egypt, France, Greece, Italy, New Zealand, Portugal, South Africa, Turkey, UK, USA, USSR
PRODUCTION:	6472 Mk Vs

As the first Spitfire variant to see extensive service outside of Britain, the Mk V fought the Axis alliance not only on the Western Front, but over North Africa, the Mediterranean, Australasia, and the Eastern Front. The first attempts by Supermarine to upgrade the Mk I/II had resulted in the production of two Mk IIIs, the latter fighter boasting a 1390 hp Merlin XX, revised airframe, stronger undercarriage, clipped wings and a retractable tailwheel. However, all these improvements combined to slow down the production rate of the desperately needed fighter, so an order for 1000 was cancelled, and the much simpler Mk V was chosen instead. Getting the improved aircraft into the frontline was a matter of great importance, as the arrival of new German fighters (the Bf 109F and the Fw 190A) on the Channel front had rendered the early marks ineffective. In order to speed up the delivery process, the Mk V had been created by simply pairing a Mk I or II fuselage with the new Merlin 45 engine – the combination proved to be so successful that some 6479 airframes would eventually be built. Thanks to this overwhelming production run, the Mk V bore the brunt of fighter operations on virtually all fronts to which the RAF was committed between 1941 and late 1943. ∎

PETER WYKEHAM-BARNES

Peter Wykeham-Barnes was born on 13 September 1915 at Sandhurst in Surrey, and he joined the RAF as a Halton apprentice in 1932. He was then selected to become a Cadet at the RAF College, Cranwell, and graduated in 1937.

When war began in Egypt in June 1940, Wykeham-Barnes flew the only Hurricane (P2639) in North Africa forward to Mersa Matruh on attachment to No 33 Sqn. Flying P2639 on a patrol near Sollum with four No 33 Sqn Gladiators, he engaged a formation of nine Fiat CR.42s and quickly shot down the leader with a short burst at full deflection while the Italian pilot was performing a vertical turn. In the fierce fight which ensued, Wykeham-Barnes hit a second, which was also confirmed – the first of his 17 kills, three of which were shared. On returning to No 80 Sqn, he resumed flying the Gladiator, gaining two more victories on 4 August, when he himself was obliged to bail out. Engaging the Italians once again four days later, he brought down yet another CR.42 with his Gladiator, and in the process become an ace.

Soon afterwards Wykeham-Barnes became a founder member of No 274 Sqn, formed as the first all-Hurricane unit in Egypt – he made his first claims with the squadron on 9 December. Shortly before leaving No 80 Sqn, he had become the first fighter pilot in North Africa to receive a DFC. Receiving a Bar to his DFC in August, he became Wing Commander Fighters, Western Desert, in November, until being rested and then sent to the USA as an air-fighting instructor.

Wykeham-Barnes later commanded No 257 Sqn when it converted, from Hurricanes to Typhoons, and in 1942 took over No 23 Sqn – flying Mosquito II intruders – which he led to Malta, where he gained his final victories. After staff tours in the UK, he joined the 2nd Tactical Air Force, commanding a Mosquito Wing with distinction.

Wykeham-Barnes remained in the RAF post-war, his final appointment was as Deputy Chief of Air Staff. Peter Wykeham-Barnes passed away in 1995.

GLADIATOR I L8009 OF FLG OFF PETER WYKEHAM-BARNES, NO 80 SQN, SIDI BARRANI, EGYPT, AUGUST 1940

Wykeham-Barnes attacked and shot down a Ba.65 of 159º Squadrigilia on 4 August 1940 to claim No 80 Sqn's first victory of World War 2.

AIRCRAFT SPECIFICATION
Gladiator I

TYPE:	single-engined biplane fighter
ACCOMMODATION:	one pilot
DIMENSIONS:	length 27 ft 5 in (8.36 m) wingspan 32 ft 3 in (9.83 m) height 10 ft 4 in (3.15 m)
WEIGHTS:	empty 3450 lb (1565 kg) maximum take-off 4750 lb (2155 kg)
PERFORMANCE:	maximum speed 253 mph (407 kmh) range 428 miles (689 km) powerplant Bristol Mercury VIIIA/AS or IX output 840 hp (626 kW)
ARMAMENT:	four BSA Colt Browning 0.303-in machine guns on the sides of the forward fuselage and under the wings
FIRST FLIGHT DATE:	12 September 1934
OPERATOR:	Belgium, China, Egypt, Eire, Finland, Greece, Iraq, Latvia, Lithuania, Norway, Portugal, South Africa, Sweden, UK
PRODUCTION:	768

The ultimate (and final) British biplane fighter of them all, the Gladiator started life as a company private venture, Gloster basing its new SS.37 (as the Gladiator was designated) very much on its predecessor, the Gauntlet. Although equipped with four guns, the design still embraced the 'old' technology of doped fabric over its wood and metal ribbed and stringered fuselage and wings. Following its first flight in September 1934, the Gladiator I was swiftly put into production, with Gloster eventually building 231 examples. It made its service debut in January 1937, and went on to fly with 26 RAF fighter squadrons. The later Mk II was fitted with the Bristol Mercury VIIIA engine, and 252 new-build machines were delivered – a number of Mk Is were also upgraded to this specification through the fitment of the later powerplant. Sixty arrestor-hooked Sea Gladiators were also built for the Royal Navy, plus a further 165 Mk I/IIs for foreign export customers. A considerable number of Gladiators were still in service when war broke out in September 1939, and although obsolete, they gave a good account of themselves in North Africa, the Middle East, over Malta and in East Africa. ■

DONALD McGEE

Born in Brooklyn, New York, on 15 July 1920, Donald Charles McGee became an aviation cadet on 30 April 1941 joining the 8th Pursuit Group as a pilot in late December 1941. Shipped out with the rest of the group to help defend Australia, in late April 1942, the 8th PG was posted north to Seven-Mile Strip on the outskirts of the New Guinean capital, Port Moresby, a key target for the Japanese.

Donald McGee had a dream start to his combat career, downing one of nine Zeros that he engaged on his first mission on 1 May 1942 – this was also the first of 453 victories that would be credited to the now redesignated 8th Fighter Group (FG) by war's end. He added two more Zeros to his tally on 29 May, bouncing the fighters from above some 50 miles southeast of Port Moresby.

Transferring to the P-38-equipped 80th FS towards the end of 1942, McGee claimed his fourth victory on 12 April 1943 when he destroyed a 'Betty' bomber heading for Port Moresby. His all-important fifth kill came over Wewak on 15 September when he downed a 'Tony' fighter. Two months later McGee, now a captain, returned home after completing his 154-mission tour. Spending the next nine months instructing tyro fighter pilots on the P-47, McGee succeeded in getting back into combat with a posting to the Eighth Air Force's P-51D-equipped 363rd FS/357th FG, based in England. Arriving in the late summer, he eventually became CO of the 363rd, and then the 364th FS. McGee scored his final aerial kill on 2 March 1945 in a 363rd FS P-51D when he downed a Bf 109 near Magdeburg, in Germany.

Remaining in the air force post-war, he was promoted to lieutenant colonel on 1 June 1952 and eventually retired from the USAF in October 1967.

P-39D-1 41-38338 NIP'S NEMESIS II OF 2LT DON C McGEE, 36TH FS/8TH FG, PORT MORESBY, NEW GUINEA, JUNE 1942

One of the few P-39 pilots to have more than one victory confirmed during the 8th FG's initial combat deployment to New Guinea, 'Fibber' McGee still maintains that he downed at least five aircraft with the Airacobra in 1942. One of those unconfirmed kills was officially recorded as a probable (a Zero attacked on 5 May near Port Moresby), while another unspecified engagement saw McGee credited with having damaged a Japanese aircraft. In any event, his single Zero kill on 1 May, followed by a pair of Mitsubishi fighters 28 days later, were officially recognised. It remains unclear whether McGee scored any of his victories with this particular P-39, which was assigned to him after the original Nip's Nemesis was damaged beyond repair during the engagement of 1 May.

AIRCRAFT SPECIFICATION
Bell P-39D Airacobra

TYPE:	single-engined monoplane fighter
ACCOMMODATION:	one pilot
DIMENSIONS:	length 30 ft 2 in (9.19 m) wingspan 34 ft 0 in (10.36 m) height 11 ft 10 in (3.61 m)
WEIGHTS:	empty 5645 lb (2560 kg) maximum take-off 8300 lb (3765 kg)
PERFORMANCE:	maximum speed 386 mph (621 kmh) range 650 miles (1046 km) powerplant Allison V-1710-85 output 1200 hp (895 kW)
ARMAMENT:	one American Armament Corporation T-9 37 mm cannon and two Colt-Browning 0.50-in machine guns in the nose, two or four Colt-Browning 0.30-in machine guns in the wings and one 500-lb (227 kg) bomb on an external rack
FIRST FLIGHT DATE:	6 April 1938 (XP-39)
OPERATOR:	France, Italy, Portugal, UK, USA, USSR
PRODUCTION:	9594

Bell's revolutionary P-39 introduced the concept of both the centrally-mounted powerplant and the tricycle undercarriage to single-engined fighters, the aircraft's unusual configuration stemming from its principal armament, the propeller hub-mounted T-9 37 mm cannon. In order to allow the weapon to be housed in the nose the P-39's engine was moved aft to sit virtually over the rear half of the wing centre-section. This drastically shifted the aircraft's centre of gravity, thus forcing designers to adopt a tricycle undercarriage. Unfortunately, the P-39's radical design was not matched by stunning performance figures particularly at heights exceeding 14,000 ft, its normally-aspirated Allison V-1710 struggling in the 'thinner' air at these altitudes – following a service evaluation of the YP-39 in 1938–39, Bell was told by USAAC and NACA officials that a turbocharged version of the V-1710 then available for the Airacobra was not needed! Once the fighter entered service in 1941 the wisdom of this decision was quickly called into question. Indeed, so compromised was the aircraft's 'combatability' in its designated role that it was soon relegated to close air support duties in theatres where other aircraft could be employed as fighters. Operating at much lower altitudes over the eastern front, the Soviet air force did, however, achieve great aerial success with the Bell fighter, utilising some 5000 from 1942 onwards. ∎

JACK STOREY

William Storey, usually known as 'Jack', was born in Victoria, Australia, on 15 November 1915. Commencing his teaching career in 1935, he volunteered for the RAAF without hesitation upon the outbreak of war. Sent to Canada to earn his wings, Storey completed his training in England and then joined No 135 Sqn in September 1941. The unit was posted to Burma shortly afterwards. Storey made his first claim following his first operational sortie, and by the end of February he had four confirmed and two probables to his name, and had been promoted to flight commander. By the time the retreat from Burma ended, he had flown over 60 hours on operations in the most desperate conditions in less than a month.

Jack Storey remained with No 135 Sqn as it rebuilt, and in early 1943 he took part in offensive sweeps down the Arakan Peninsula toward Akyab. During the morning of 5 March 1943, he led a patrol over the Japanese-held port at 21,000 ft, engaging the enemy as he later recalled:

'The Japs split up and during the dogfight, which soon took us down to 12,000 ft, more appeared and joined in. After much tail chasing I finally got an opening and carried out a downward quarter attack on a straggler and got in a beautiful deflection shot... It rolled over and went straight down through clouds, streaming petrol vapour from the port wing tank...' Storey then led his men back to the landing ground at Ritz, where his fifth victory was confirmed. After refuelling, 'A' Flight returned to Akyab, where Storey found that they were well positioned to jump a vic of 'Oscars' where he secured another three kills.

Storey was awarded the DFC on 9 April 1943. In early May he claimed his eighth, and last, victory, and soon afterwards was posted to an instructional job. He was repatriated to Australia in 1944, where he undertook further instructional work until his demobilisation after the war. Storey then completed his degree and returned to teaching until his retirement.

HURRICANE IIB Z5659/WK-C OF PLT OFF WILLIAM J STOREY, NO 135 SQN, MINGALADON, BURMA, FEBRUARY 1942

On 6 February 1942 the Japanese attacked Mingaladon airfield, on the outskirts of Rangoon, and Jack Storey scrambled in this aircraft, leading six others aloft. Three Ki-27 'Nate' fighters of the 77th Sentai jumped them, and in the subsequent fight Storey shot down two and claimed two probables. He was again flying Z5659 on 23 February when he sent a 'Nate' into the jungle in flames for his fourth victory. Storey's faithful Hurricane was eventually struck off charge on 7 July 1943.

AIRCRAFT SPECIFICATION
Hawker Hurricane Mk II

TYPE:	single-engined monoplane fighter
ACCOMMODATION:	one pilot
DIMENSIONS:	length 32 ft 3 in (9.83 m) wingspan 40 ft 0 in (12.19 m) height 13 ft 3 in (4.04 m)
WEIGHTS:	empty 5658 lb (2566 kg) maximum take-off 7490 lb (3397 kg)
PERFORMANCE:	maximum speed 324 mph (521 kmh) range 460 miles (740 km) powerplant Rolls-Royce Merlin 24 output 1620 hp (1193 kW)
ARMAMENT:	eight Browning 0.303-in machine guns in wings
FIRST FLIGHT DATE:	11 June 1940
OPERATOR:	Australia, Belgium, Canada, Eire, Finland, France, India, The Netherlands, Portugal, South Africa, UK, USSR, Yugoslavia
PRODUCTION:	8406

On 11 June 1940 a Hurricane Mk I airframe was flown with a two-stage supercharged Merlin XX engine fitted in place of the Merlin III. Designated the Hurricane Mk II, deliveries of the machine to frontline units commenced in September of that year. The first Series 1 Mk IIs retained the standard wings of the Hurricane Mk I, but the Series 2 machines boasted fuselage strengthening to allow the fitment of wings featuring universal attachment points for external stores. An extra fuselage bay was also incorporated into the machine, increasing the fighter's overall length by seven inches. The 12-gun Mk IIB was produced from late 1940, and the following year the four 20 mm cannon Mk IIC also made its service debut. All Mk II variants had underwing attachments for bombs, rockets, drop tanks and other external stores. Although deemed obsolescent for the day-fighter role in the UK, the Hurricane II continued to serve as a fighter-bomber and night intruder on the Channel Coast into 1943. In North Africa, the Mediterranean and the Far East, the Hurricane was the most modern fighter available to the RAF. The aircraft, in its Sea Hurricane guise, was also the primary carrier-based fighter in service with the Fleet Air Arm in 1941–42. Although Hurricane production finally ceased in September 1944, the aircraft remained in frontline service in the Far East until VJ-Day. ■

CLIVE CALDWELL

Born in 1911, Clive Robertson Caldwell joined the RAAF upon the outbreak of war and was among the first RAAF-trained pilots to join Tomahawk-equipped No 250 Sqn, then based at Aqir, in Palestine, four months later.

Caldwell later recalled his thoughts on the various models of P-40 he flew;

'Of the two I preferred the Tomahawk as a pilot's aircraft, favouring only the greater lethal density of the Kittyhawk's six 0.50 calibre guns. The aeroplane handled and turned well, recovered from a spin without fuss and in general had little vice.'

Caldwell performed his first operational patrol on 14 May, and soon afterwards moved to the Western Desert, where he achieved great success during intensive operations. On 26 June Caldwell, in AK419, downed the Bf 109E flown by Leutnant Heinz Schmidt of I./JG 27 – the first of his eventual 30 victories, including three shared, which made him the leading RAAF ace of World War 2. Caldwell's aggression quickly earned him the nickname of 'Killer', something he personally detested, as fellow ace 'Bobby' Gibbes recalled:

'Clive was given the name "Killer" (which was not of his choosing, or liking) due to his habit of shooting up any enemy vehicle which he saw below when returning from a sortie. Invariably, he landed back at his base with almost no ammunition left.'

Caldwell became the first Commonwealth pilot to claim five victories flying the P-40. He was promoted to command the elite No 112 Sqn, flying Kittyhawks, with whom he achieved further victories, before leaving for Australia. Upon returning home, Caldwell was given command of the first RAAF Spitfire wing, which he led with distinction in the defence of Darwin in 1943, and with whom he personally destroyed eight Japanese aircraft. Awarded a DSO, he eventually left the RAAF as a group captain in 1946. He passed away in 1994.

TOMAHAWK IIB AK498 OF FLT LT CLIVE CALDWELL, NO 250 SQN, LG 123 MADDELENA NO 3, LIBYA, NOVEMBER–DECEMBER 1941

Clive Caldwell of No 250 Sqn became the first Commonwealth ace to claim five victories on the Tomahawk, achieving this feat on 7 July. In November he was assigned this aircraft, which carried his 'scoreboard'. On 23 November he used AK498 to destroy two Bf 109s, but his outstanding feat with it came on 5 December when he was credited with downing five Ju 87s. His ninth, and final, confirmed claim with AK498 was on 20 December, when another Bf 109 fell to him. On Christmas Eve Caldwell also used this machine to damage the Bf 109F of 69-victory experte Oberleutnant Erbo Graf von Kageneck of III./JG 27, who later died of his wounds. AK498 was also used by future ace Plt Off John Waddy to make his first confirmed claim on 9 December. This aircraft was struck off charge on 1 April 1944.

AIRCRAFT SPECIFICATION
Curtiss P-40B/C Tomahawk

TYPE:	single-engined monoplane fighter
ACCOMMODATION:	one pilot
DIMENSIONS:	length 31 ft 8.5 in (9.66 m) wingspan 37 ft 3.5 in (11.37 m) height 10 ft 7 in (3.22 m)
WEIGHTS:	empty 5812 lb (2636 kg) maximum take-off 8058 lb (3655 kg)
PERFORMANCE:	maximum speed 345 mph (555 kmh) range 1230 miles (1979 km) with external drop tank powerplant Allison V-1710-33 output 1040 hp (775 kW)
ARMAMENT:	two Colt-Browning 0.50-in machine guns in the nose and two or four 0.30-in machine guns in the wings
FIRST FLIGHT DATE:	14 October 1938
OPERATOR:	Australia, Canada, China, Egypt, South Africa, Turkey, UK, USA, USSR
PRODUCTION:	1703

The Curtiss P-40 series of fighters was a progressive development of the company's earlier radial-engined P-36, which had been ordered in substantial numbers by the USAAC and the French l'Armée de l'Air. There was clearly development potential in the airframe, and this duly led to the production of a variant fitted with an Allison inline engine. France contracted for the type as the Hawk H-81, which the US designated the P-40. The British Purchasing Commission also issued an initial contract for the fighter, which was named Tomahawk in RAF service after the war axe used by the North American Indians. Trials showed that the Tomahawk would be unsuitable for service in the fighter role over Europe, and indeed the early Mk Is were woefully armed. However, it was decided that the better armed Mk IIBs should re-equip fighter squadrons in the Middle East, this decision following the December 1940 rejection of the Tomahawk by Fighter Command after the latter had conducted brief trials with several Mk IIAs. Later fitted with more powerful engines and increased armament, the aircraft, from the P-40D series onwards, was known as the Kittyhawk. As such, it was to see widespread and distinguished service with the Commonwealth air forces in many theatres, ranging from the blazing heat of North Africa to the steamy jungles of New Guinea and the Solomons. Initially, the Curtiss machine was used in the fighter role, but later it served to great effect as a fighter-bomber until war's end. Almost 50 pilots from the Commonwealth air forces claimed five or more victories flying it, and nearly 40 more aces made at least part of their 'score' on the type. ∎

WALTER NOWOTNY

One of the many Austrians to rise high in the ranks of the wartime Luftwaffe, Walter Nowotny flew almost exclusively against the Russians. He was arguably the most successful Fw 190 pilot on the Eastern Front, with 258 confirmed kills.

He joined III. Gruppe of JG 54 in February 1941, and his first three victories – a trio of I-153 biplanes claimed over the Baltic Sea on 19 July of that year – were very nearly his last. Forced to ditch, the 20-year-old Nowotny barely survived the following 72 hours in an open dinghy before being washed ashore. By the autumn of 1942 his scored had topped the 50 mark, he had been awarded the Knight's Cross, and he was serving as the Staffelkapitän of 1./JG 54.

In June 1943 Nowotny claimed 41 kills, including ten in one day. In August he was made Gruppenkommandeur of I./JG 54, and he celebrated his promotion by scoring 49 victories during this month alone! In September his tally reached 200, and on 14 October 1943 he became the first Luftwaffe fighter pilot to achieve 250 kills. Nowotny was honoured with the Diamonds to the Oak Leaves with Swords of his Knight's Cross.

Nowotny's stunning tally was derived from a mixture of exceptional flying skills and intense bravery. In one encounter he described a classic fighting manoeuvre:

> Throughout the chase I have been slipping to the right in an attempt to dodge my pursuer's shots. I try the same manoeuvre one last time. And this time Ivan falls for it. For a split-second, as I wallow once more to the right at little more than a stall, he loses concentration. I take two more cannon hits before I complete the manoeuvre, but then he has overshot me, flashing past beneath my wings. He appears ahead of me… I ram home the throttle – full power! Within a trice I am on top of the Russian. He goes down under my first burst of fire.

In the autumn of 1944, following a spell commanding a fighter training school, Major Nowotny was selected to head an experimental Me 262 jet fighter unit but was killed on 6 November while engaging US bombers.

FW 190A-4 'WHITE 8' OF LEUTNANT WALTER NOWOTNY, STAFFELKAPITÄN 1./JG 54, KRASNOGVARDEISK, NOVEMBER 1942

A well-documented machine, in stark contrast to the majority of the anonymous and unidentifiable Fw 190s flown on the Eastern Front by all and sundry (or at least by whoever's name happened to be next on the ops board), this is the aircraft in which Nowotny scored his Staffel's 300th victory of the war. The toned-down – or simply dirty – white of the fuselage cross seems an unnecessary precaution on an otherwise standard white winter camouflaged A-4.

AIRCRAFT SPECIFICATION
Focke-Wulf Fw 190A
(all dimensions and performance data for Fw 190A-3)

TYPE:	single-engined monoplane fighter
ACCOMMODATION:	one pilot
DIMENSIONS:	length 29 ft 0 in (8.84 m) wingspan 34 ft 5.5 in (10.50 m) height 13 ft 0 in (3.96 m)
WEIGHTS:	empty 6393 lb (2900 kg) maximum take-off 8770 lb (3978 kg)
PERFORMANCE:	maximum speed 382 mph (615 kmh) range 497 miles (800 km) output 1700 hp (1268 kW)
ARMAMENT:	two 7.9 mm machine guns in nose, four 20 mm cannon in wings
FIRST FLIGHT DATE:	June 1, 1939
OPERATOR:	Germany, Turkey
PRODUCTION:	19379 (all models)

Arguably Germany's best piston-engined fighter of the war, the Fw 190 caught the RAF by surprise when it appeared over the Channel Front in 1941. Indeed, the Focke-Wulf fighter remained unmatched in aerial combat in the west until the advent of the Spitfire Mk IX in late 1942 and the La-5FN and Yak-9 on the Eastern Front in early 1943. Powered by the compact BMW 801 radial engine, the Fw 190 also boasted excellent handling characteristics to match its turn of speed. A-model Fw 190s were the dedicated fighter variants of the 'butcher bird', and as the design matured, so more guns were fitted and more power squeezed out of the BMW engine. By the end of 1942, production of the Fw 190 accounted for half of all German fighters built that year, and the fighter-bomber F/G had also been developed – the first F-models entered frontline service on the Eastern Front during the winter of 1942–43. All manner of ordnance from bombs to rockets could be carried by the fighter-bomber Fw 190, and additional protective armor for the pilot was also added around the cockpit. Variants of the Fw 190 saw action against the Allies on all fronts of the war in Europe, and the aircraft remained a deadly opponent for Allied fighter pilots right up to VE-Day. ■

PETE BROTHERS

Lancastrian Peter Malam 'Pete' Brothers joined No 32 Sqn at RAF Biggin Hill in October 1936, where he flew Gauntlet II biplane fighters until the first Hurricane Is arrived at the No 11 Group station exactly two years later. By then a highly experienced fighter pilot, and flight commander, Brothers first saw action as a result of the German Blitzkrieg into Western Europe in May 1940. Embroiled in the Battle of Britain following the surrender of France, he remained in the thick of the action by joining No 257 Sqn in early September following No 32 Sqn's posting out of the frontline. Flt Lt Brothers was awarded a Distinguished Flying Cross (DFC) just prior to leaving his beloved No 32 Sqn.

With his score standing at 12 kills, Brothers briefly served as an instructer in early 1941 before being promoted to squadron leader and tasked with forming the Australian-manned No 457 Sqn, equipped with Spitfires. He was to see continual service in Supermarine fighters throughout the remaining war years during a succession of frontline postings, leading No 602 Sqn in 1942, the Tangmere Wing the following year and finally the Exeter and Culmhead Wings in 1944. By VE-Day, now Wg Cdr Brothers had increased his score to 16 destroyed, 1 probable and 3 damaged, and been awarded a bar to his DFC and a Distinguished Service Order (DSO).

Post-war, he remained in the RAF until retiring with the rank of air commodore in 1973. Several years later, Brothers was subsequently elected Master of the Guild of Air Pilots and Air Navigators, his City of London Livery Company. He remained very active within the Battle of Britain Pilots' Association for several decades and campaigned for the Battle of Britain memorial now on the Thames Embankment in London. He passed away in 2008 at the age of 91.

HURRICANE MK I P2921/'GZ-L' OF FLT LT 'PETE' BROTHERS, NO 32 SQN, BIGGIN HILL/ HAWKINGE, JULY 1940

This Hurricane was one of three Hawker fighters sent to No 32 Sqn on 11 June 1940 as attrition replacements for the trio of aircraft lost by the unit in combat during a patrol over Le Tréport 48 hours earlier. As the newest of the three to arrive at Biggin Hill, P2921 was immediately 'acquired' by 'B' Flight commander, 'Pete' Brothers. He flew P2921 throughout July and August 1940, during which time he was credited with destroying eight German aircraft (six Bf 109Es, a Bf 110 and a Do 17). The fighter remained with No 32 Sqn until 21 February 1941, when it was transferred to the newly formed No 315 'Polish' Sqn at Speke, near Liverpool.

AIRCRAFT SPECIFICATION
Hawker Hurricane Mk I

TYPE:	single-engined monoplane fighter
ACCOMMODATION:	one pilot
DIMENSIONS:	length 31 ft 5 in (9.58 m) wingspan 40 ft 0 in (12.19 m) height 13 ft 0 in (3.96 m)
WEIGHTS:	empty 4982 lb (2260 kg) maximum take-off 7490 lb (3397 kg)
PERFORMANCE:	maximum speed 324 mph (521 kmh) range 600 miles (965 km) powerplant Rolls-Royce Merlin I/II/III output 1030 hp (768 kW)
ARMAMENT:	eight 0.303-in machine guns in wings
FIRST FLIGHT DATE:	6 November 1935
OPERATOR:	Australia, Belgium, Canada, Finland, France, The Netherlands East Indies, Romania, South Africa, UK, Yugoslavia
PRODUCTION:	3843

The Hurricane's arrival in the frontline in December 1937 saw the RAF finally make the jump from biplane to monoplane fighter. The aircraft owed much to Hawker's ultimate biplane design, the Fury, both types being built around an internal 'skeleton' of four wire-braced alloy and steel tube longerons – this structure was renowned for both its simplicity of construction and durability. The Hurricane also benefited from Hawker's long-standing partnership with Rolls-Royce, whose newly-developed Merlin I engine proved to be the ideal powerplant. Toting eight 0.303-in machine guns, and capable of speeds in excess of 300 mph, the Hurricane I was the world's most advanced fighter when issued to the RAF. Although technically eclipsed by the Spitfire come the summer of 1940, Hurricanes nevertheless outnumbered the former type during the Battle of Britain by three to one, and actually downed more Luftwaffe aircraft than the Supermarine fighter. Even prior to its 'finest hour', Hurricanes provided the first RAF aces of the war in France during the Blitzkrieg. In 1940/41 the Mark I saw action in the Mediterranean and East and North Africa, fighting valiantly against numerically superior Italian forces. Finally, in 1942, a veritable handful of tropicalised Hurricane Is attempted to halt the Japanese invasion of the Far East, the fighter seeing action over Singapore, Malaya, Burma and Java. Although the last Mk I was built in 1941, later Hurricane variants remained in production until September 1944. ■

GÜNTHER RALL

The third of the Jagdwaffe's trio of 'top three' scorers – after Erich Hartmann's 352 and Gerhard Barkhorn's 301 – Günther Rall claimed 275 aircraft destroyed, all but three of them on the Eastern Front and all of them while flying a Bf-109. Born in Gaggenau, Baden, on 10 March 1918, Rall's military career had begun as an officer-cadet with Infantry Regiment 13, and he had then transferred to the Luftwaffe. Posted to 8./JG 52 just prior to the outbreak of war, Rall achieved his first kill (a Curtiss Hawk 75) on 18 May 1940.

He was appointed Staffelkapitän of 8./JG 52 in July, but like Hartmann and Barkhorn, he would fail to score against the RAF, and it was not until the campaign in the east that Rall, too, came into his own. On 28 November 1941, after claiming a pair of I-16s near Rostov, he was seriously injured in a crash-landing. His back broken in three places and in a plaster cast for many months, it was late in July 1942 before he rejoined his Staffel. He was determined to return to active duty as he later recalled, 'When I crashed I had 36 kills. I returned to flying in August 1942 and was quite eager to get going again. I felt I had lost much time.' Rall claimed kill 65 on 2 September, for which he was awarded the Knight's Cross the following day. On 22 October he reached his century, and received the Oak Leaves four days later.

Assuming command of III. Gruppe in July 1943, Rall became the third pilot to reach the 200 mark (on 29 August 1943), which earned him the Swords, and the second to achieve 250. In April 1944, with 273 kills under his belt, he was transferred to Defence of the Reich duties as Kommandeur of II./JG 11. Here, he would claim just two more victories. On 12 May Rall scored his 275th, and final, kill of the war – a P-47 east of Koblenz – but he was himself severely injured during the dogfight. Made Geschwaderkommodore of JG 300 in early 1945, Rall and his compatriots operated from a number of different airfields throughout southern Germany but during the final days of the war instructed his men to attempt to stay alive rather than to carry out senseless actions. Eventually captured by American forces he spent some months as a PoW following VE-Day.

He joined the newly-formed Bundesluftwaffe in the 1950s, and was instrumental in helping to push through Germany's controversial F-104 programme – he duly led the Starfighter-equipped JaboGeschwader 34. After attaining the topmost rank in the Bundesluftwaffe (Chief of the Air Staff), Günther Rall's last position before retirement, in 1975, was as a member of the NATO Military Committee. He passed away at his home in Germany in 2009 at the age of 91.

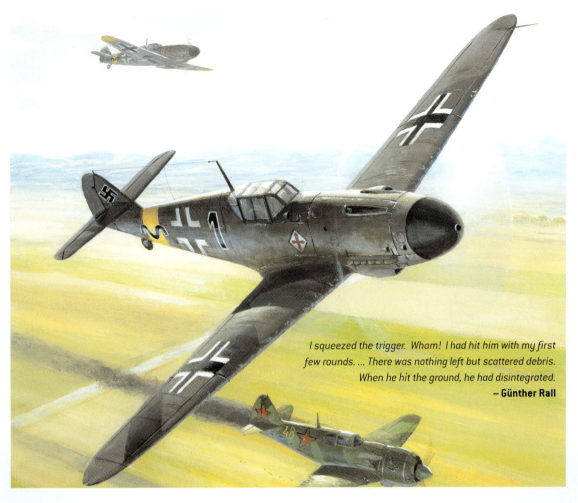

I squeezed the trigger. Wham! I had hit him with my first few rounds. ... There was nothing left but scattered debris. When he hit the ground, he had disintegrated.
— Günther Rall

BF 109G-2 'BLACK 13' OF OBERLEUTNANT GÜNTHER RALL, STAFFELKAPITÄN 8./JG 52, GOSTANOVKA, RUSSIA, AUGUST 1942

Oberleutnant Günther Rall flew 'Black 13' upon his return to the command of 8. Staffel on 28 August 1942, exactly nine months to the day after being severely wounded the previous November. At that time he had claimed just 36 kills. He would add 235 more Soviet victories to his score (latterly as Kommandeur of III./JG 52) before his transfer to the west in the spring of 1944. Note III. Gruppe's 'Barbed cross' badge forward of the windshield and the wavy bar symbol on the aft fuselage. This particular machine has long been associated with Günther Rall, although he flew it only occasionally. His usual mount at this time, in accordance with his position as Staffelkapitän, was 'Black 1'.

AIRCRAFT SPECIFICATION
Messerschmitt Bf 109G-6

TYPE:	single-engined monoplane fighter
ACCOMMODATION:	one pilot
DIMENSIONS:	length 29 ft 7.5 in (9.03 m) wingspan 32 ft 6.5 in (9.92 m) height 8 ft 2.5 in (2.50 m)
WEIGHTS:	empty 5893 lb (2673 kg) maximum take-off 7496 lb (3400 kg)
PERFORMANCE:	maximum speed 386 mph (621 kmh) range 620 miles (998 km) with external tank powerplant Daimler-Benz DB 605AM output 1800 hp (1342 kW)
ARMAMENT:	one Rheinmetall Borsig MK 108 20 mm cannon in propeller hub and two Rheinmetall Borsig MG 131 13 mm machine guns in upper cowling, two Mauser MG 151 20 mm cannon in underwing gondolas; provision for various underfuselage and underwing stores
FIRST FLIGHT DATE:	late summer 1941
OPERATOR:	Bulgaria, Croatia, Finland, Germany, Hungary, Italy, Rumania, Slovakia, Switzerland, Spain
PRODUCTION:	approximately 24,000 G-models and around 750 K-models

The Bf 109G combined the F-model's refined airframe with the larger, heavier and considerably more powerful 1475 hp DB 605 engine to produce the most successful Messerschmitt fighter variant of them all. Cockpit pressurisation was also introduced for the first time with the G-1, although most later sub-variants lacked this feature. Produced in staggering numbers from early 1942 until war's end, more than 24,000+ Bf 109G/Ks were constructed in total – including an overwhelming 14,212 in 1944. Numerous modifications to the basic G-1 were introduced either in the factory (as Umrüst-Bausätze factory conversion sets) or in the field (Rüstsätze), and these included provision for extra armament, additional radios, introduction of a wooden tailplane, the fitting of a lengthened tailwheel and the installation of the MW50 water/menthanol-boosted DB 605D engine. In an attempt to standardise the equipment of the frontline force, Messerschmitt produced the Bf 109G-6 in late 1942, and this model included many of these previously ad hoc additions. Unfortunately, the continual addition of weighty items like wing cannon and larger engines to the once slight airframe of the Bf 109 eliminated much of the fighter's manoeuvrability, and instead served to emphasise the aircraft's poor low speed performance, lateral control and ground handling. The final variant to enter widespread service with the Luftwaffe was the Bf 109K-4. ∎

ROY WHITTAKER

Roy 'Deke' Whittaker is remembered as the leading ace of the 57th FG, one of the USAAF's most storied units of World War 2. Born in Knoxville, Tennessee, on 6 July 1919, Roy Eugene Whittaker graduated from the University of Tennessee prior to joining the US Army Air Corps on 15 March 1941. His leadership abilities stood out from the beginning, as he was appointed Commandant of Cadets of Class 41-I, completing flight training at Kelly Field, Texas, on 12 December 1941 – less than a week after the United States entered World War 2. He transferred to the recently formed 57th PG, which was training for combat in the Curtiss P-40 Warhawk.

Lt Whittaker and the rest of the air echelon of the 57th left for North Africa aboard the aircraft carrier USS *Ranger* in June 1942. Arriving off the Gold Coast port of Accra in early July, the 57th FG promptly made history by becoming the first USAAF fighter group to launch at strength from an aircraft carrier. Whittaker's P-40F Warhawk was the second of 72 aeroplanes off *Ranger*'s deck that day. After a brief period flying with the RAF to gain combat experience, Whittaker commenced full-scale operations with the 57th FG when the El Alamein offensive opened in late October 1942. The future ace destroyed an Italian C.202 for his first aerial victory on 26 October, and added a second Italian fighter to his score the following day. His first victory over a German aircraft – a Bf 109G – came on 11 January 1943.

Recently promoted to captain, Whittaker took part in the famous 'Palm Sunday Massacre' mission of 18 April 1943, shooting down three Ju 52/3m transports and a Bf 109 off Cape Bon, Tunisia, a critical event in the Tunisian campaign:

> I attacked the Ju 52s from astern at high speed and fired at two aeroplanes in the leading formation. The bursts were short, and the only effect I saw were pieces flying off the cabin of the second ship. I pulled away, circled to the right and made my second attack. I fired two bursts into two more Ju 52s, again in the leading formation. They both burst into flames… I then made a third pass and sent a good burst into the left of the formation of another Junkers. As I pulled away, it crashed into the water. By that time the Me 109s were among us. As I pulled up to the left, I saw a '109 dive through an element of four Warhawks and I tagged on his underside and gave him a long burst in the belly. He crashed into the sea from 1000 ft.
>
> I then joined up with some Warhawks that were carrying Lufberying with six Me 109s. I met one of these fighters with a quartering attack and hit him with a short burst. Pieces flew from the aeroplane and he started smoking, but climbed out of the fight. It was a fighter pilot's dream.

This brought his score to seven confirmed victories, which was the highest total amassed by any 57th FG pilot during the war. Whittaker completed his combat tour in June 1943, having flown 87 combat missions. He saw out the rest of the war as an instructor in the US.

Post-war, Whittaker became a career US Air Force officer, retiring in 1973 with the rank of colonel. He died on 24 June 1989.

I attacked the Ju 52s from astern at high speed... I fired two bursts into two more Ju 52s, again in the leading formation. They both burst into flames.
– Roy Whittaker

P-40F-1 41-14081 'WHITE 43' OF CAPT ROY E 'DEKE' WHITTAKER, 65TH FS/57TH FG, HANI MAIN, TUNISIA, APRIL–MAY 1943

Whittaker, top ace of the 57th FG, flew two similarly-marked Warhawks during his combat tour, and this was the second of them. The first was transferred to the 66th FS in December 1942 and renumbered 'White 96'. This aeroplane carries Whittaker's full score of seven victories, and it also displays the 65th FS 'Fighting Cocks' badge on the nose. Note that swastikas have been used to mark all of Whittaker's kills, although two of his victims were Italian aircraft. His most successful combat mission was on 18 April 1943, when he shot down three Ju 52/3m transports and a Bf 109 during the 'Palm Sunday Massacre'.

AIRCRAFT SPECIFICATION
Curtiss P-40F/L Kittyhawk/Warhawk

TYPE:	single-engined monoplane fighter
ACCOMMODATION:	one pilot
DIMENSIONS:	length 33 ft 4 in (10.16 m) wingspan: 37 ft 4 in (11.38 m) height 12 ft 4 in (3.76 m)
WEIGHTS:	empty 7000 lb (3175 kg) maximum take-off 8500 lb (3855 kg)
PERFORMANCE:	maximum speed 364 mph (586 kmh) range 1500 miles (2414 km) with external drop tank powerplant Packard Merlin V-1650-1 output 1300 hp (1104 kW)
ARMAMENT:	six Colt Browning 0.50-in machine guns in the wings; one 500-lb (227 kg) bomb under the fuselage or two 100-lb (45 kg) under the wings
FIRST FLIGHT DATE:	30 June 1941
OPERATOR:	Australia, South Africa, UK, USA, USSR
PRODUCTION:	2000

The poor performance of the Allison-engined P-40 at altitudes in excess of 20,000 ft had been a cause of great concern to the Allies from the start of the war. In an attempt to solve this problem, Curtiss re-engined the second production P-40D airframe with a Rolls-Royce Merlin 28. Flown for the first time on 30 June 1941 (as the XP-40F), the fighter's performance was deemed to have been improved sufficiently enough for orders for 1311 P-40Fs to be placed. These were powered by Packard-built V-1650-1 Merlins, rated at 1300 hp for take-off. Boasting a similar six-gun armament to the Allison-engined P-40E/K, the F-model also subsequently adopted the lengthened fuselage of the P-40K-10. An order for 330 P-40Fs was placed with Curtiss for Commonwealth air forces, and some 117 of these were supplied to the RAF, Royal Australian Air Force (RAAF) and the South African Air Force (SAAF), with 100 of the remaining airframes going to the USSR. The final Merlin-engined variant was the P-40L, which had two guns removed and its fuel capacity reduced in an effort to save overall weight – 700 L-models were built. Some 300 surviving P-40F/Ls were re-engined with Allison V-1710-81s and redesignated P-40Rs in 1944 because of a shortage of Merlin spares. P-40F/Ls saw action with the Allies in North Africa and the Mediterranean, the Far East, the Pacific and on the eastern front. ■

LAWRENCE 'PINKIE' STARK

Born in Bolton, Lancashire, 'Pinkie' Stark joined the RAF in 1940 midway through an apprenticeship with Metropolitan-Vickers in Manchester. Trained in Canada, he served as a Staff Pilot at No 10 Air Gunnery School upon his return to the UK in mid-1941. Helping air gunners achieve proficiency with turret gun-firing, Stark flew Defiants in this rather unglamorous role for a full year, before being posted to No 56 Operational Training Unit. He joined No 609 Sqn in early 1943, and subsequently became one of the few aces to score all his kills flying Typhoons.

Awarded a DFC in March 1944, Stark had by then been posted to No 263 Sqn, where he served as a flight commander until shot down by flak over Brittany on 3 July. He evaded capture, and upon his return to the UK was sent to Gloster Aircraft Company to serve as a production test pilot on Typhoons. A Bar to his DFC was announced during September of 1944. Having been sufficiently rested, Stark was sent back to the frontline in March 1945, serving initially as a flight commander with No 164 Sqn, and then assuming command of No 609 Sqn.

Following the auxiliary unit's disbandment in September 1945, he performed staff duties in Germany before joining the Aeroplane & Armament Experimental Establishment. Stark was employed as a test pilot at Boscombe Down for over three years, before resuming frontline flying as a flight commander with No 32 Sqn in the Middle East. More test flying followed this squadron tour, and he eventually retired from the RAF in November 1963. In civilian life, 'Pinkie' Stark managed Rochester Airport for 25 years, before retiring to live in nearby Bredhurst, near Gillingham. He passed away in 2004.

TYPHOON MK IB SW411/'PR-J' OF SQN LDR L W F STARK, OC NO 609 SQN, PLANTLUNNE (B.103), GERMANY, MAY 1945

Having completed a tour with No 609 Sqn in 1943–44, 'Pinkie' Stark returned to the unit in March 1945 as its last wartime commanding officer. For much of his time with the squadron, he retained SW411 as his personal aircraft, flying his first mission in it on 19 March 1945 and his last in September when No 609 Sqn disbanded. The gloss black and yellow spinner worn by this aircraft was applied soon after VE-Day. The inner surfaces of the undercarriage doors were also finished in yellow, with white edging. Stored at No 5 MU at Kemble for a year, SW411 was finally scrapped in October 1946.

AIRCRAFT SPECIFICATION
Hawker Typhoon Mk IB

TYPE:	single-engined monoplane fighter
ACCOMMODATION:	one pilot
DIMENSIONS:	length 31 ft 11 in (9.73 m) wingspan 41 ft 7 in (12.67 m) height 15 ft 3.5 in (4.66 m)
WEIGHTS:	empty 9800 lb (4445 kg)
PERFORMANCE:	maximum speed 412 mph (659.2 kmh) range 980 miles (1577 km) with external tanks powerplant Napier Sabre IIA output 2180 hp (1626 kW)
ARMAMENT:	four 20 mm cannon in wings; provision for two 500-lb (227-kg) or 1000-lb (454-kg) bombs or eight 3-in/60-lb (7.62-cm/27-kg) rockets under wings
FIRST FLIGHT DATE:	24 February 1940
OPERATOR:	Canada, New Zealand, UK
PRODUCTION:	3317

The Typhoon was the RAF's first production fighter capable of achieving speeds in excess of 400 mph in level flight. However, the brutish Hawker design was almost deemed a failure right at the start of its career when the combination of poor climb and altitude performance, unreliability of its new Napier Sabre engine (chosen in favour of the cancelled Rolls-Royce Vultee/Hawker Tornado combination) and suspect rear fuselage assembly cast serious doubts over its suitability for frontline service. Refusing to give up on the aircraft, Hawker and Napier spent over a year (from mid-1941 through to mid-1942) 'beefing up' the airframe and correcting engine maladies to the point where the Typhoon was found to be an excellent low altitude fighter – it effectively neutralised the Luftwaffe's Fw 190 'hit and run' raiders, which had frequently terrorised the south coast of England in 1942–43. The Typhoon's proven ability at low-level also made it the ideal platform for the ground-attack mission, its quartet of 20 mm cannon and deadly array of rockets and bombs allowing pilots to roam the skies over occupied western Europe attacking all manner of targets from ships to tanks. One of the key weapons in the Allied arsenal for Operation *Overlord*, the Typhoon equipped more than 20 units by mid 1944. The last example of Hawker's original Napier-engined fighter was built in November 1945. ∎

HIROYOSHI NISHIZAWA

Born on 27 January 1920, in Nagano Prefecture, Hiroyoshi Nishizawa joined the navy in June 1936 and completed flying training in March 1939. When the Pacific War began, Nishizawa was flying Japanese Naval Air Force (JNAF) Type 96 'Claudes' with the Chitose Air Group (AG) in the Marshall Islands, and he duly accompanied the group to Rabaul, where he joined the 4th AG in February 1942. When elements of the Tainan AG arrived at Rabaul from the Dutch East Indies in April, Nishizawa was transferred into the 2nd Squadron, where he found himself in the company of PO1/c Saburo Sakai. The latter tutored the gaunt and sickly loner, together with PO2/c Toshio Ota, and together the threesome became famous as the 'Cleanup Trio'. In November, surviving pilots of the Tainan AG were transferred to the 251st, with those few who had survived the combats over Guadalcanal being held in high esteem by the JNAF. In September the 251st AG was re-rolled as a nightfighter unit, and PO1/c Nishizawa was transferred to the 253rd AG, based at Tobera Airfield (Rabaul). The following month he was ordered back to Japan to serve as an instructor as part of the JNAF's efforts to cure their fighter pilot shortage.

He hated his new assignment, likening it to baby-sitting, and after repeated requests for a combat assignment, he was transferred to the 201st AG in the Philippines in time to participate in the counter-attack against the American naval fleets. From June through to 21 August 1943, CPO Nishizawa would engage new US F4U Corsairs on a regular basis as the Allies pushed northwards towards Rabaul. During this period, he participated in the destruction of 45 Corsairs, which were attributed to his unit rather than to him as individual victory credits were prohibited.

With an eventual tally of 86 kills, Nishizawa graphically proved just how effective the Mitsubishi A6M Type 0 was in skilled hands. He was eventually killed when the transport bomber he was a passenger in was shot down on 26 December 1944 when he was en route to pick up some replacement Zeros.

A6M3A MODEL 22 OF CPO HIROYOSHI NISHIZAWA, 251ST AG, AICHI PREFECTURE, JAPAN, EARLY SPRING 1943

The unit designation 'UI' was used from 1942 through to June 1943, during which time Hiroyoshi Nishizawa flew this aircraft as an instructor. The standard JNAF light gray scheme worn by this fighter was hastily camouflaged with foliage green paint within days of the 251st arriving in Rabaul.

AIRCRAFT SPECIFICATION
Mitsubishi A6M2/3 Zero
(all dimensions and performance data for A6M2 Model 21)

TYPE:	single-engined monoplane fighter
ACCOMMODATION:	one pilot
DIMENSIONS:	length 29 ft 8.75 in (9.06 m) wingspan 39 ft 4.25 in (12.00 m) height 10 ft 0.15 in (3.05 m)
WEIGHTS:	empty 3704 lb (1680 kg) maximum take-off 6164 lb (2796 kg)
PERFORMANCE:	maximum speed 331 mph (533 kmh) range 1930 miles (3105 km) with external tanks powerplant Nakajima NK1C Sakae 12 output 950 hp (708 kW)
ARMAMENT:	two 7.7 mm machine guns in nose, two 20 mm cannon in wings; provision for two underwing 132-lb (60-kg) bombs
FIRST FLIGHT DATE:	1 April 1939
OPERATOR:	Japan
PRODUCTION:	4335

Undoubtedly the most famous Japanese combat aircraft of World War 2, the A6M was developed by Mitsubishi to meet a demanding JNAF requirement for a replacement to the successful A5M of the late 1930s. Officially designated the Navy Type O Carrier Fighter Rei-sen ('Zero Fighter'), the A6M offered an impressive mix of high performance, long range and superb manoeuvrability, all in a lightweight and modestly powered airframe. The first two prototype A6M1s were powered by the relatively underpowered and undeveloped Mitsubishi Zuisei 13 engine, and a switch was soon made to the Sakae, which it retained until war's end. Redesignated the A6M2, the first production-standard Model 11s were delivered to the JNAF in July 1940, and barely two months later the variant saw action over China when 13 Zeros tangled with 27 Polikarpov I-15s and I-16s and shot them all down without suffering a single loss! Production switched to the Model 21 at around the same time, this variant having folding wingtips for deck elevator compatibility. A6M2s made up no less than two-thirds of the JNAF's fighter force by December 7, 1941, and 135 Zeros took part in the Pearl Harbor assault. By then the re-engined A6M3 was just entering production, the new variant being powered by a supercharged Sakae 21 rated at 1130 hp (843 kW). This variant also dispensed with the folding wingtips, leaving the wings with a 'squared off' appearance. A6M3 production finally ended in mid 1943. ∎

WILLIAM 'BILL' LEVERETTE

A native of Palatka, Florida, Bill Leverette joined the army reserve in September 1934, having obtained a degree in mechanical engineering prior to signing up. He served in the infantry until 1939, when he transferred to the Army Air Corps. Rated a pilot in March 1940, Leverette flew P-39s with the 31st Pursuit Group and 53rd and 338th Fighter Groups in the USA, before transferring to the 14th FG in North Africa in August 1943.

By this stage a very experienced pilot, but having yet to test his mettle in combat, Leverette joined the 37th FS, flying P-38 Lightnings. And despite having seen no action, he was made CO of the unit just weeks after his arrival in the Mediterranean Theater of Operations (MTO). He had little real affection for the big Lockheed fighter, which he claimed was tiring to fly, but nevertheless enjoyed great success during his tour. On 9 October 1943 Leverette achieved a record score for a USAAF pilot in a single mission. In his first encounter with the enemy, the major claimed seven aircraft destroyed and two damaged with the two flights of P-38Gs he was leading spotted a large formation of Ju 87D Stukas over the island of Rhodes. The Stukas proved to be easy pickings for the American pilots. Aside from the seven Ju 87Ds that he destroyed on 9 October, Leverette also claimed two Bf 110s and two Bf 109s before leaving the 14th FG in April 1944.

He remained in the post-war air force, rising to the rank of full colonel. Bill Leverette finally retired from the USAF in December 1965.

P-38H (SERIAL UNKNOWN) 'STINGEREE' OF MAJ WILLIAM L LEVERETTE, CO OF THE 37TH FS/14TH FG, GAMBUT-2, LIBYA, OCTOBER 1943

Named after a southern American variation of the stingray, this P-38H was used by Bill Leverette to claim most, if not all, of his 11 aerial victories. The seven Ju 87s that he was credited with on 9 October 1943 constituted a record for American pilots in Europe. This astounding tally has often been questioned by ex-pilots and historians alike, but Leverette assured Osprey author John Stanaway that one of the P-38 pilots in his formation descended to low altitude over the becalmed sea in order to confirm numerous splashes in the water made by the crashing Stukas. Once the latter individual had returned to base, the number of splashes he reported was consistent with the tally of kills claimed by the successful P-38 pilots.

AIRCRAFT SPECIFICATION
Lockheed P-38H Lightning

TYPE:	single-engined monoplane fighter
ACCOMMODATION:	one pilot
DIMENSIONS:	length 37 ft 10 in (11.53 m) wingspan 52 ft 0 in (15.85 m) height 9 ft 10 in (3.00 m)
WEIGHTS:	empty 12,380 lb (5615 kg) maximum take-off 20,300 lb (9208 kg)
PERFORMANCE:	maximum speed 402 mph (643.2 kmh) range 2400 miles (3840 km) with external tanks powerplants two Allison V-1710-89/-91 engines output 2850 hp (2126 kW)
ARMAMENT:	one 20 mm cannon and four 0.50 in machine guns in nose; maximum bomb load of 4000 lb (1814 kg) under wings
FIRST FLIGHT DATE:	27 January 1939 (XP-38)
OPERATOR:	USA
PRODUCTION:	601 (including 128 F-5C photo-recce variants)

The P-38 Lightning was Lockheed's first venture into the world of high-performance military aircraft in response to the USAAC's 1937 Request for Proposals for a long-range interceptor. Aside from its novel twin-boom and central nacelle layout, the prototype XP-38 utilized butt-joined and flush-riveted all-metal skins (and flying surfaces) – a first for a US fighter. The XP-38's test program progressed well, and aside from some minor adjustments to the flying surfaces and introduction of progressively more powerful Allison engines, frontline P-38s differed little from the prototype throughout the aircraft's six-year production run. The appellation 'Lightning' was bestowed upon the P-38 by the RAF when the type was ordered in 1940, and duly adopted by the Americans the following year. The near-identical G- and H-model P-38s proved to be the real workhorse variants of the Lightning in the MTO, being issued to Twelfth and Fifteenth Air Force fighter groups from the autumn of 1943 onwards. Used primarily as bomber escorts, the Lockheed fighters roamed all over the Mediterranean thanks to the aircraft's impressive range. And no fewer than 37 aces scored five or more kills in the MTO with the Lightning, making it the most successful fighter in-theatre in 1943–44. ∎

HERMANN GRAF

For the fighter pilot who was the first in the world to score 200 kills, who received Germany's highest decoration when a 29-year-old Oberleutnant, and who ended the war as Kommodore of JG 52 (the most successful fighter unit ever in terms of aerial victories), the name of Hermann Graf is now surprisingly little known to all but a few.

Although he joined JG 51 in the early months of the war, a subsequent stint as a fighter instructor meant that Leutnant Graf did not achieve his first victory until August 1941 when serving with JG 52 on the Eastern Front. But within little over a year after that, he was wearing the Diamonds – awarded on 16 September 1942 for 172 aircraft destroyed. Graf was one of only seven day fighter pilots so honoured.

By now a national hero, the one-time apprentice blacksmith was able to indulge his life-long passion for football. Graf formed his own team, 'The Red Hunters', and whenever he was posted to a new unit he ensured that his star players accompanied him as techical experts! In this way some of Germany's greatest post-war football players were spared frontline service.

In 1943 Graf served another spell in training command, before heading the specialist unit JG(r) 50 and JG 11 in Defence of the Reich duties. JG 11 was equipped with some of the first rocket-armed Bf 109G-6s. This netted him ten heavy bombers before he returned to JG 52 in the east in October 1944, this time as Kommodore. By war's end he had amassed a total of 212 aerial victories. He and the rest of JG 52 surrendered to US forces on 8 May 1945 but were handed over to the Red Army.

It was during the immediate post-war years of Soviet captivity that the pragmatic Graf's actions contributed to his own downfall. Unlike others, such as the redoubtable Erich Hartmann, Graf co-operated – some say collaborated – with his captors. After his release in 1950 and return to Germany, he was ostracised by many of his former comrades. Although most have since mellowed, Hermann Graf has been fated to remain something of a 'non-person' in Luftwaffe history. He died in his home town of Engen, in Baden, in November 1988, aged 76.

BF 109G-6 (WK-NR 15913) 'RED 1' OF MAJOR HERMANN GRAF, GRUPPENKOMMANDEUR JG(R) 50, WIESBADEN-ERBENHEIM, SEPTEMBER 1943

This G-6 Kanonenboot was the mount of Major Hermann Graf during his tenure of office as Kommandeur of the single Gruppe-strong JG(r) 50 in the late summer/early autumn of 1943. The rudder meticulously records all of Graf's Eastern Front victories, the number 172 (for which he received the Diamonds), surmounted and surrounded by his initials and the award ribbon, plus two rows of 15 individual bars each. The last three bars are for recent western successes, including the two B-17s downed on 6 September. Hermann Graf would claim a total of ten four engined bombers in Defence of the Reich operations before returning to the east, and his old unit, JG 52.

A simply fantastic scene unfolds before my eyes. My own two [air-to-air] rockets both register a perfect bull's-eye on a Fortress. Thereupon, I am confronted with an enormous solid ball of fire.
– Hermann Graf

AIRCRAFT SPECIFICATION
Messerschmitt Bf 109G-6

TYPE:	single-engined monoplane fighter
ACCOMMODATION:	one pilot
DIMENSIONS:	length 29 ft 7.5 in (9.03 m) wingspan 32 ft 6.5 in (9.92 m) height 8 ft 2.5 in (2.50 m)
WEIGHTS:	empty 5893 lb (2673 kg) maximum take-off 7496 lb (3400 kg)
PERFORMANCE:	maximum speed 386 mph (621 kmh) range 620 miles (998 km) with external tank powerplant Daimler-Benz DB 605AM output 1800 hp (1342 kW)
ARMAMENT:	one 20 mm cannon in propeller hub, two 13 mm machine guns in upper cowling and two 20 mm cannon under wings; provision for various underfuselage and underwing stores
FIRST FLIGHT DATE:	late summer 1941
OPERATOR:	Bulgaria, Croatia, Finland, Germany, Hungary, Italy, Romania, Slovakia, Switzerland
PRODUCTION:	23,500 G-models

The Bf 109G combined the F-model's refined airframe with the larger, heavier and considerably more powerful 1475 hp DB 605 engine to produce the most successful Messerschmitt fighter variant of them all. Cockpit pressurisation was also introduced for the first time with the G-1, although most later sub-variants lacked this feature. Produced in staggering numbers from early 1942 until war's end, some 23,500 Bf 109Gs were constructed in total – including an overwhelming 14,212 in 1944. Numerous modifications to the basic G-1 were introduced either in the factory (as Umrüst-Bausätze factory conversion sets) or in the field (Rüstsätze), and these included provision for extra armament, additional radios, introduction of a wooden tailplane, the fitting of a lengthened tailwheel and the installation of the MW50 water/methanol-boosted DB 605D engine. In an attempt to standardise the equipment of the frontline force, Messerschmitt produced the Bf 109G-6 in late 1942, and this model included many of these previously ad hoc additions. Unfortunately, the continual adding of weighty items like wing cannon and a larger engine to the once slight airframe of the Bf 109 eliminated much of the fighter's manoeuvrability, and instead served to emphasise the aircraft's poor low speed performance, lateral control and ground handling. ∎

EUGENIUSZ HORBACZEWSKI

Eugeniusz Horbaczewski was born in 1917 in Kiev. He was known throughout his life as 'Dziubek' (an informal Polish word which in English means 'darling' or 'kid'). He joined the air force flying school at Deblin in 1938, and was commissioned in the 13th Promotion on 1 September 1939.

Upon reaching France, Horbaczewski apparently flew with a Polish flight at Bordeaux before fleeing once again to Britain in June 1940 and obtaining a posting to No 303 Sqn. Always ready for action, he was a tough subordinate, and in September 1942 Sqn Ldr Jan Zumbach had him posted away to No 302 Sqn following a series of minor incidents which eventually resulted in a Spitfire being written off. Apparently it was then that Dziubek swore he would exceed Zumbach's score!

Horbaczewski then joined the Spitfire-equipped Polish Fighting Team in North Africa, and in six months scored eight kills. Whilst in the MTO he rose through the ranks from flying officer to squadron leader, and was eventually given command of No 43 Sqn.

Upon returning to Britain, Horbaczewski was made OC No 315 Sqn which was equipped with Mustang IIIs and part of No 133 Wing, which was led by ranking Polish ace Stanislaw Skalski. Ironically, in mid-1944 Dziubek found himself under the command of Jan Zumbach once again after the latter replaced Skalski as Wing Leader – further irony was provided when Horbaczewski finally fulfilled his oath soon after the command change.

Throughout the summer of 1944, the Polish-manned No 315 Sqn used the extensive range of the Mustang IIIs to roam across Occupied Europe from Normandy to Norway. One of the most successful long-range missions flown by the unit took place on 30 July 1944, when six Mustang IIIs downed eight German fighters off the Norwegian coast. Horbaczwski's report from that combat reads as follows:

> While escorting Beaufighters over the Norwegian coast on July 30th at 1555 hrs, we met about 15 ME 109s and attacked them. We were above them and the MEs were apparently not expecting to see single-engined fighters so far north, as they took no evasive action, possibly mistaking us for other ME 109s. I dived down on them and gave one a three-second burst, after which he caught fire and went straight into the sea. I climed up, and when climbing I spotted another ME 109 below me. I came down and gave him a long burst. Strikes were seen in the cockpit and on the wings, glycol began to leak from the enemy aircraft, and it was losing speed and height. My guns jammed so I formated on him and started calling by R/T my No 2 (Flg Off Bozydar Nowosielski). The enemy aircraft had no hood and I could see that the pilot's face was covered in blood, and he put up his hands. He was heading towards the Norwegian coast, so I ordered my No 2 to open fire.

Dziubek himself was killed on 18 August 1944 during an air battle which saw his squadron credited with 16 Fw 190s destroyed – he downed three of them prior to his death. He was unwell that day, and some witnesses claim that he knew he would not survive an encounter with German fighters.

I dived down on them and gave one a three-second burst, after which he caught fire and went straight into the sea.
— Eugeniusz Horbaczewski

MUSTANG III FB166/PK-G OF SQN LDR EUGENIUSZ DZIUBEK HORBACZEWSKI, OC NO 315 SQN, BRENZETT, JUNE 1944

This aircraft had been ferried from Aston Down to No 315 Sqn by Sgt Tamowicz on 13 April 1944, and subsequently became Horbaczewski's personal mount. On 12 June Dziubek flew the Mustang on a successful sortie fresh from an inspection at the Coolham-based No 411 (Polish) Repair & Salvage Unit (RSU), claiming an Fw 190 destroyed before being hit by flak. He then flew the fighter directly back to No 411 RSU for repairs to be effected! FB166 was soon back with No 315 Sqn, and on 30 July Horbaczewski enjoyed more success with it off the Norwegian coast. Following its eventful spell in the frontline, the Mustang III then spent time with No 61 OTU at Rednal in early 1945, before being allocated to Polish-manned No 316 Sqn at Andrews Field, in Essex, in the last weeks of the war. FB166 was finally struck off charge in December 1946.

AIRCRAFT SPECIFICATION
North American Mustang III

TYPE:	single-engined monoplane fighter
ACCOMMODATION:	one pilot
DIMENSIONS:	length 32 ft 3 in (9.83 m) wingspan 37 ft 0 in (11.28 m) height 13 ft 8 in (4.16 m)
WEIGHTS:	empty 6980 lb (3166.12 kg) maximum take-off 11,800 lb (5352.48 kg)
PERFORMANCE:	maximum speed 439 mph (702.4 kmh) range 2700 miles (4320 km) with external tanks powerplant Packard V-1650-3 output 1380 hp (1019 kW)
ARMAMENT:	six 0.50-in machine guns in wings; up to 2000 lb (907 kg) bombs or six 5-in (12.7-cm) rocket projectiles under wings
FIRST FLIGHT DATE:	13 October 1942
OPERATOR:	China, UK, USA
PRODUCTION:	770+ Mustang IIIs supplied to the RAF through Lend-Lease

Early RAF Mustang operations had seen the aircraft restricted to fighter-reconnaissance and army co-operation duties due to the poor altitude performance of the fighter's Allison engine. Some 800+ Mk I/IA/IIs had been supplied to the air force in 1941/42, and they remained in service until war's end. The mating of the Merlin engine with the airframe in late 1942 resulted in the production of the P-51B/C for the AAF and the Mustang III for the RAF. The first examples of the revitalised North American fighter were issued to No 19 Sqn in February 1944, and by VE-Day no fewer than 18 ETO-based units had re-equipped with the Mustang III. Six squadrons also saw considerable action with the fighter in the Mediterranean Theatre of Operations (MTO) during the final year of the war. Many of the units serving in the European Theatre of Operations (ETO) were assigned to the 2nd Tactical Air Force for much of 1944, during which time they escorted bombers operating in support of the D-Day invasion of France and flew close-support missions for troops on the ground. The Mustang III also exacted a heavy toll on the pilotless V1 'Doodlebugs' fired against south-east England in mid-1944 – the aircraft was credited with the destruction of 232 flying bombs. By this stage in the war, few manned German aircraft were being encountered in the areas in which the Mustang III operated, but seven pilots nevertheless scored five or more kills in the fighter. The Mk III was slowly replaced in frontline service by the P-51D/K-derived Mk IV from late 1944 onwards. ∎

CHARLES McCORCKLE

A graduate of the army's prestigious West Point Military Academy, Charles McCorkle was commissioned a second lieutenant in the field artillery in June 1936. He soon decided on a career in aviation, however, for he was rated a pilot at Kelly Field, Texas, in early October of that same year! McCorkle transferred to the Army Air Corps exactly 12 months later, and over the next five years accrued much experience serving as both a fighter pilot and an instructor.

In June 1942 he was posted to the 54th FG in Alaska, which was embroiled in the fight for the Aleutians at the time. Flying P-39s, McCorkle was given command of the group three months after his arrival in-theatre, and he subsequently led the outfit back to the USA at the end of 1942. In the spring of the following year the 54th FG became the first AAF group to receive P-51B Mustangs, after which its trio of squadrons were redesignated replacement training units.

By now a full colonel, McCorkle was transferred to the MTO in August 1943 to oversee the transition of the 31st FG onto the North American fighter. This group had been flying the Spitfire since its arrival in Europe in the autumn of 1942, and with Mustangs not available until March 1944, its new CO would get ample opportunity to become familiar with the superlative British fighter. McCorkle had 'made ace' by early February, and he continued to claim victories with the P-51B until he completed his tour in July 1944.

'Sandy' McCorkle remained in the air force post-war, rising to the rank of major-general by the time he retired in 1966.

P-51B-10 42-106501 'BETTY JANE' OF COL CHARLES M McCORKLE, CO OF THE 31ST FG, SAN SEVERO, ITALY, JUNE 1944

It was the group CO's prerogative to use his own initials instead of a conventional three-letter code, thus McCorkle had the codes 'CM-M' painted on his aircraft, repeating the letters 'CM' on the nose. The 31st FG otherwise used the same codes as the 78th FG in Britain, which was a deliberate duplication aimed at confusing the enemy. The group initially adorned its aircraft with a single diagonal red stripe as its distinguishing marking, before five parallel diagonal stripes, covering the entire tailfin, rudder and tailplanes, took its place. McCorkle was already an ace when the 31st replaced its much-loved Spitfires Mk VIIIs with Mustangs, the colonel subsequently adding six P-51 kills to the five he had previously scored flying the British fighter.

AIRCRAFT SPECIFICATION
North American P-51B-5 Mustang

TYPE:	single-engined monoplane fighter
ACCOMMODATION:	one pilot
DIMENSIONS:	length 32 ft 3 in (9.83 m) wingspan 37 ft 0 in (11.28 m) height 13 ft 8 in (4.16 m)
WEIGHTS:	empty 6980 lb (3166.12 kg) maximum take-off 11,800 lb (5352.48 kg)
PERFORMANCE:	maximum speed 439 mph (702.4 kmh) range 2700 miles (4320 km) with external tanks powerplant Packard V-1650-3 output 1380 hp (1019 kW)
ARMAMENT:	six 0.50-in machine guns in wings; up to 2000 lb (907 kg) of bombs or six 5-in (12.7-cm) rocket projectiles under wings
FIRST FLIGHT DATE:	13 October 1942
OPERATOR:	China, UK, USA
PRODUCTION:	1988

Four groups operated P-51B/Cs within the recently-formed Fifteenth Air Force from March 1944 through to the early spring of 1945. The Spitfire-equipped 31st and 52nd FGs became the first groups to receive examples of the North American fighter, followed by the 325th and 332nd FGs, both of which gave up P-47Ds. The aircraft soon made its presence felt in the MTO, for on 21 April the 31st FG claimed 17 enemy aircraft destroyed while escorting heavy bombers sent to bomb the oilfields at Ploesti, in Romania. Perhaps the aircraft's single most outstanding achievement came on 31 August when the 52nd FG attacked the Luftwaffe airfield at Reghin, again in Romania, and destroyed over 150 aircraft in an orgy of destruction. Serving primarily as bomber escorts for the burgeoning ranks of B-17 and B-24 'heavies' tasked with knocking out strategic targets in Germany, Austria and the Balkans, pilots within the four Mustang groups saw plenty of action – indeed, no fewer than 50 of them achieved sufficient kills to be classified as aces. By early 1945 most 'razorback' P-51B/Cs had been replaced by the definitive P-51D/K, and the North American fighter remained a familiar sight in southern European skies until VE-Day. ■

WILLI MAXIMOWITZ

Unlike the other famous and highly decorated Luftwaffe fighter aces so vividly portrayed in the dramatic artwork within this volume, Willi Maximowitz remains a shadowy and virtually unsung figure. His inclusion serves to represent that solid core of NCO pilots – many of them veterans of long years' standing – who provided the backbone of the wartime Jagdwaffe, and who contributed so much to their units' successes.

Little is known of Maximowitz's operational career, if any, prior to his service as a Sturm pilot. Although not among the 18 original pilots who formed Sturmstaffel 1 in November 1943, he was one of the second intake of volunteers who joined the unit a few weeks later. Unteroffizier Maximowitz's first victory – a B-24 brought down on 30 January 1944 – was the result of just such an action. He would score three more kills, all B-17s, before the pioneering Sturmstaffel was absorbed into IV.(Sturm)/JG 3 in the late spring of 1944.

Flying with the Gruppe's 11. Staffel, Maximowitz added seven more 'heavies' to his total, but was then severely injured when his Sturmbock ('Battering Ram') overturned on landing on 30 July. He returned to operations in late September, now as a Schwarmführer (leader of a four-aircraft section) in 14. Staffel. Before the year was out, his tally had risen to 15.

Early in 1945 IV.(Sturm)/JG 3 was transferred to the Eastern Front, and Feldwebel Maximowitz's last dozen kills were all Russian. A recipient of the German Cross in Gold (an award which ranked just below the Knight's Cross), Maximowitz and his entire Schwarm were reported missing after last being seen under attack by Soviet fighters east of Berlin on 20 April 1945.

FW 190A-8/R8 'BLACK 8' OF UNTEROFFIZIER WILLI MAXIMOWITZ, IV.(STURM)/JG 3, SALZWEDEL, CIRCA JUNE 1944

Unlike the majority of the anonymous A-8/R8s flown by this specialist unit, Willi Maximowitz's 'Sturmböck' featured JG 3's 'Winged U' badge and the IV.Gruppe wavy bar marking. 'Black 8' was reportedly one of the aircraft deployed briefly to Normandy. If this is the case, and in view of its gaudy paint scheme, both it and Maximowitz were lucky to survive! A member of the original Sturmstaffel 1, Maximowitz's final tally is uncertain, one source quoting 25 kills, 15 of which were 'heavies' (several destroyed by ramming).

AIRCRAFT SPECIFICATION
Focke-Wulf Fw 190A-8

TYPE:	single-engined monoplane fighter
ACCOMMODATION:	one pilot
DIMENSIONS:	length 29 ft 4.25 in (8.95 m) wingspan 34 ft 5.5 in (10.50 m) height 12 ft 11.5 in (3.95 m)
WEIGHTS:	empty 7650 lb (3470 kg) maximum take-off 9656 lb (4380 kg)
PERFORMANCE:	maximum speed 402 mph (647 kmh) range 643 miles (1035 km) powerplant BMW 801D-2 output 1700 hp (1268 kW)
ARMAMENT:	two 7.9 mm machine guns in nose, four 20 mm cannon in wings (A-8/R8 'Sturmbock' had outer 20 mm cannon replaced with 30 mm cannon)
FIRST FLIGHT DATE:	1 June 1939
OPERATOR:	Germany
PRODUCTION:	1334

The final production A-series Fw 190, the A-8 featured a new radio, repositioned fuselage bomb rack and space for an internal auxiliary fuel tank. As with previous models of the Focke-Wulf fighter, myriad Umrüst-Bausätze (factory conversion sets) and Rüstsätze (field conversion sets) enabled the basic A-8 to be modified for specialist roles such as bomber attack, ground attack and Wilde Sau nightfighting. The A-8 also formed the basis for the Sturmbock, which equipped IV.(Sturm)/JG 3 in the spring of 1944. This aircraft featured both additional armour-plating around the cockpit and ammunition boxes and extra panels of laminated glass on the sides of the canopy in an effort to protect the pilot from the bombers' heavy calibre machine gun fire. The A-8/R8 also packed a hefty punch, with single MK 108 30 mm cannon being fitted in the outer wing stations in place of the standard MG 151 20 mm weapons. The former's high-explosive shells proved extremely destructive at short range, with combat experience showing that, on average, a heavy bomber could be brought down with just three 30 mm rounds. The heavy weight of the cannon and the additional armour plating made the Sturmbock far less agile than a standard A-8, however, and when engaged by escorting American fighters the Sturm pilot had little chance to defend himself. ■

CLARENCE 'BUD' ANDERSON

A native of Oakland, California, 'Bud' Anderson entered the Army Air Corps' Aviation Cadet Program in January 1942, being rated a pilot some nine months later at Luke Field, Arizona. Initially assigned to the P-39-equipped 328th FG, 2Lt Anderson flew defensive patrols along the Pacific coast from Oakland Municipal Airport, in the San Francisco Bay area. Some months later he became a founder member of the 363rd FS, which was part of the equally new 357th FG that had been activated at Tonopah, in the Nevada desert, on 1 December 1942. As with the 328th FG, this new group was also assigned Airacobras. Anderson was sent overseas with the 357th in late November 1943.

The 357th FG was destined to become the first fighter group in the Eighth Air Force to be equipped with the Merlin-engined Mustang, commencing operations from Leiston, in Suffolk, in February 1944. 'Bud' Anderson soon proved his ability in combat, and by the time his first combat tour came to an end in July, his score stood at 12.25 victories. Following a spell on leave in the USA, he returned to complete a second tour, raising his final tally to 16.25 kills. Anderson had flown 116 missions in less than a year, and had never been hit by enemy fire or aborted a sortie.

Remaining in the air force postwar, he spent time as a test pilot, commanded the Sabre-equipped 69th FBS in Korea in the mid-1950s and saw action over Vietnam in the F-105 Thunderchief whilst in command of the 355th TFW in 1970. Col Anderson retired from the USAF in 1972 to join McDonnell Aircraft Company, and he subsequently served for 12 years with the aerospace giant at Edwards AFB as manager of its flight test facility.

P-51D-10 MUSTANG 44-14450/'OLD CROW' OF CAPT CLARENCE E 'BUD' ANDERSON, 363RD FS/357TH FG, LEISTON, NOVEMBER 1944

Despite the P-51D being present at Leiston from May 1944 onwards, 'Bud' Anderson had flown a B-model Mustang throughout his first tour. He explained why in his autobiography: 'The Ds had begun arriving in the spring of 1944, and I got my own when I came back from leave. I could have had one of the first ones in May, but my earlier B-model was working so well, and I was so close to the end of my tour, that rather than take some new airplane and shake all the bugs out, I decided to stay with the "Old Crow" I had.' Anderson claimed four Fw 190s destroyed and two as probables flying 44-14450.

AIRCRAFT SPECIFICATION
North American P-51D/K Mustang

TYPE:	single-engined monoplane fighter
ACCOMMODATION:	one pilot
DIMENSIONS:	length 32 ft 3 in (9.83 m) wingspan 37 ft 0 in (11.28 m) height 12 ft 2 in (3.71 m)
WEIGHTS:	empty 7635 lb (3463 kg) maximum take-off 12,100 lb (5488 kg)
PERFORMANCE:	maximum speed 437 mph (703 kmh) range 1650 miles (2655 km) with external tanks powerplant Packard V-1650-7 output 1720 hp (1283 kW)
ARMAMENT:	six 0.50 in machine guns in wings; up to 2000 lb (907 kg) of bombs or six 5 in (12.7 cm) rocket projectiles under wings
FIRST FLIGHT DATE:	17 November 1943
OPERATOR:	Australia, China, the Netherlands, New Zealand, South Africa, UK, USA
PRODUCTION:	9493

The P-51D was effectively an improved version of the B/C-model that had first been fitted with the Merlin 61 engine in late 1942. One of the major complaints from Eighth Air Force fighter pilots who debuted the revised Mustang in combat in early 1944 centered on the poor rearward visibility on offer. North American quickly set about rectifying this with the follow-on P-51D, which was designed from the outset to feature a cut-down rear fuselage and a 360-degree clear vision tear-drop canopy. The new variant also boasted an additional two 0.50 in machine guns in the wings, although the engine remained the same as was installed in late-production P-51B/Cs – the license-produced Packard V-1650-7. The first D-model Mustangs arrived in the ETO just prior to D-Day, and the aircraft had replaced all 'razorback' P-51s in-theatre by year-end. Despite its better visibility and improved armament, the newer model was not universally welcomed by all, as Lt Elmer O'Dell of the 363rd FG explained: 'I flew all of my missions in the same P-51B-10, and in June 1944 I was offered a P-51D, but I preferred to keep the B-10. I checked out the D and flew a number of mock combat missions in it, but to me it didn't have the delicate response of the B-10, which had four 0.50-calibre guns. When they built the D they added another gun to each wing. To do so, they had to alter the configuration of the wing. I maintain this caused a small reduction in manoeuvrability. I guess it was a personal thing, for obviously most pilots thought otherwise.' ∎

ERICH HARTMANN

The son of a physician, Erich Alfred Hartmann was born in Weissach, Württemberg, on 19 April 1922. Following in his father's footsteps, he intended to study medicine had the war not intervened. Instead, he left school at the age of 18 in September 1940 and joined the Luftwaffe the following month.

Hartmann was two years in training, spending time at both the cadet college in Berlin and the fighter school at Zerbst, before joining his first operational unit – 7. Staffel of JG 52 – at Soldatskaya, on the southern sector of the eastern front, in October 1942. His first victory – an Il-2 – was achieved over the Caucasus on 5 November 1942, but it would be nearly three months (27 January 1943) before he doubled his tally by downing a MiG-1 fighter. Although something of a slow starter, Hartmann claimed his first double – a brace of LaGG-3s – on 30 April 1943 to take his score into double figures. Six months later almost to the day, on 29 October 1943, Leutnant Erich Hartmann was awarded the Knight's Cross for a total of 148 kills! His star was very much in the ascendant, and multiple daily victories had become commonplace. By this time he had been appointed Kapitän of 9./JG 52, the famous 'Karaya' Staffel.

The Oak Leaves followed on 2 March 1944 for his reaching a total of 200, and the Swords on 4 July – three days after Hartmann's promotion to Oberleutnant – for 239. On 18 July he became only the fourth pilot to achieve 250 victories, and his eleven kills on 24 August took his score to 301. The first pilot in the world to be credited with a triple century, this feat earned Hartmann the Diamonds the following day. Promoted to Hauptmann on 1 September 1944, he duly took over as Staffelkapitän of the reformed 4./JG 52 a month later, and also served as acting Kommandeur of II. Gruppe. Invited to join Adolf Galland's Me 262-equipped JV 44, Hartmann declined, preferring instead to return to JG 52 on the eastern front for the remaining weeks of the war, which he saw out as Kommandeur of I. Gruppe. On 8 May 1945 – the day hostilities ceased in Europe – Erich Hartmann scored his 352nd, and last kill, and was promoted to Major.

BF 109G-6 'WHITE 1' OF HAUPTMANN ERICH HARTMANN, STAFFELKAPITÄN 4./JG 52, BUDAÖRS, HUNGARY, NOVEMBER 1944

Erich Hartmann positively advertised his presence in the air, being known to the Russians as the 'Black Devil of the South'. This is the late model G-6 flown by him after he relinquished his year-long command of 9. Staffel to set up a new 4./JG 52 in October 1944. Although the machine retains the distinctive black 'tulip-leaf' which was Hartmann's individual marking, the 'Karaya' Staffel's famous 'pierced heart' emblem below the cockpit is now a plain red heart bearing the name Usch (for Ursula, whom Hartmann had married two months previously). Note, however, there is no record of the ace's current score, which by this time was well above the 300 mark.

AIRCRAFT SPECIFICATION
Messerschmitt Bf 109G-6

TYPE:	single-engined monoplane fighter
ACCOMMODATION:	one pilot
DIMENSIONS:	length 29 ft 7.5 in (9.03 m) wingspan 32 ft 6.5 in (9.92 m) height 8 ft 2.5 in (2.50 m)
WEIGHTS:	empty 5893 lb (2673 kg) maximum take-off 7496 lb (3400 kg)
PERFORMANCE:	maximum speed 386 mph (621 kmh) range 620 miles (998 km) with external tank powerplant Daimler-Benz DB 605AM output 1800 hp (1342 kW)
ARMAMENT:	one Rheinmetall Borsig MK 108 20 mm cannon in propeller hub and two Rheinmetall Borsig MG 131 13 mm machine guns in upper cowling, two Mauser MG 151 20 mm cannon in underwing gondolas; provision for various underfuselage and underwing stores
FIRST FLIGHT DATE:	late summer 1941
OPERATOR:	Bulgaria, Croatia, Finland, Germany, Hungary, Italy, Rumania, Slovakia, Switzerland, Spain
PRODUCTION:	approximately 24,000 G-models and around 750 K-models

The highest-scoring aces in the history of aerial conflict were the Jagdwaffe pilots involved in the bloody combats on the eastern front from June 1941 through to May 1945. Men like Erich Hartmann (352 kills), Gerhard Barkhorn (301 kills) and Günther Rall (275 kills) all scored the bulk of their staggering victory tallies against the massed ranks of the Soviet Red Air Forces, with a further seven German pilots all passing the 200-mark during the campaign. The most common fighter used by these pilots was the venerable Bf 109, which was involved in the action from Operation *Barbarossa* through to the climactic Battle for Berlin in the spring of 1945. Units such as JGs 51, 52 and 54 all flew the Messerschmitt fighter in the east, progressing from the Emil to the final versions of the Gustav. Although the continual addition of weighty items such as wing cannon and larger engines to the once slight airframe of the Bf 109 had adversely affected the fighter's legendary manoeuvrability by 1943–44, the late-build G-10/14 and Bf 109K-4 were still more than a match for the latest generation of Soviet fighters at the medium to low altitudes at which most aerial action took place in the east. ■

HEINZ BÄR

In stark contrast to a number of his contemporaries, Heinz 'Pritzl' Bär's rise through the ranks was a long roller-coaster of a journey which lasted throughout the war from the first day of hostilities until the last.

Bär was a Feldwebel when he scored his first victory – a French Hawk H-75A – during the 'Phoney War'. He also flew in the Battles of France and Britain which followed, surviving the latter conflict with 17 kills to his credit. Accompanying JG 51 to Russia, the now-commissioned Leutnant Bär received the Knight's Cross for 27 victories on 2 July 1941, and was awarded the Oak Leaves six weeks later after more than doubling his total to 60.

Having increased his score to 96 kills, and added the Swords to his Oak Leaves, Heinz Bär left the Eastern Front in the spring of 1942 to take command of I./JG 77 in the Mediterranean. He was now a proven fighter leader. Fiercely supportive of those serving under him, Bär was often outspoken to the point of insubordination when it came to their welfare. This did not always endear him to his superiors.

Consequently, although he duly served as Kommodore of both JGs 1 and 3, he also spent intervening periods in more lowly positions. Towards the close of the war he converted to the Me 262 jet fighter, and the last 16 of his 220 kills – this total including 21 heavy bombers – were achieved at the controls of this revolutionary aircraft.

Heinz Bär was himself shot down no fewer than 18 times during the war. The survivor of four bail-outs and fourteen crash-landings, Bär was tragically killed in a light aircraft accident in 1957.

ME 262A-1A WK-NR 110559/'RED 13' OF OBERSTLEUTNANT HEINZ BÄR, KOMMANDEUR III./EJG 2, LAGER-LECHFELD, MARCH 1945

One of the last of a long line of 'lucky 13s' flown by Heinz Bär during a distinguished and incident-packed career, this aircraft wears an upper surface camouflage combination of dark brown and bright medium green over pale blue undersides. Beginning with a French Hawk H-75A downed on 25 September 1939, Bär had amassed 204 piston-engined aerial victories before transitioning to the Me 262, on which he scored a further 16 to become the leading daylight jet ace, and second only to the nightfighting Kurt Welter in the overall rankings.

AIRCRAFT SPECIFICATION
Messerschmitt Me 262A-1a

TYPE:	twin-engined monoplane jet fighter
ACCOMMODATION:	single-seat fighter-bomber or two-seat nightfighter
DIMENSIONS:	length 34 ft 9.5 in (10.60 m) wingspan 41 ft 0.5 in (12.51 m) height 11 ft 6.75 in (3.83 m)
WEIGHTS:	empty 9742 lb (4420 kg) normal loaded 14,101 lb (6396 kg)
PERFORMANCE:	maximum speed 540 mph (870 kmh) range 652 miles (1050 km) powerplants two Junkers Jumo 004B-1/-2 or -3 turbojet engines output 3960 lb st (17.8 kN)
ARMAMENT:	A-1a, four 30 mm cannon in nose and provision for 24 underwing rockets
FIRST FLIGHT DATE:	18 July 1942 (first all jet-powered flight)
OPERATOR:	Germany
PRODUCTION:	1433

The world's very first operational jet fighter, the Me 262 was also the most advanced aircraft of its generation to actually see combat. Design work on the Messerschmitt commenced as early as 1938, and the first tailwheeled prototype, fitted with a nose-mounted Junkers Jumo 210 piston engine, completed its maiden flight on 4 April 1941. Unfortunately for Messerschmitt, work on the aircraft's revolutionary turbojet powerplants failed to keep pace with their development of the airframe, and it was not until 18 July 1942 that the first successful flight was made with the preferred Junkers Jumo 003 turbojets installed – the BMW 003 had initially been trialled, but persistent failures had seen it discarded in early 1942. With the engine/ airframe combination at last sorted out, political interference from no less a figure than the Führer himself saw the programme side-tracked for a number of months as he insisted that the aircraft be developed as a bomber. Sense finally prevailed in early 1944, and the first aircraft to reach the frontline saw combat in June of that year. Despite Germany being bombed virtually 24 hours a day during the final 12 months of the war, 1400+ Me 262s were completed by Messerschmitt, and a further 500 were lost in air raids. Engine reliability, fuel shortages and unrealistic operational taskings restricted the frontline force to around 200 jets at any one time, but these nevertheless accounted for over 200 Allied aircraft (Jagdwaffe claims exceeded 745 victories for the Me 262!) during day and night interceptions. A total of 28 pilots 'made ace' flying the jet with the seven units that saw combat. ∎

SERGEI DOLGUSHIN

Born on 25 September 1920 in Novopokrovskoe, in the Tula Region of Russia, to a peasant family, Sergei Dolgushin worked in a factory while studying at an aeroclub in the late 1930s. Joining the army in 1939, he graduated from the Kacha Flight School the following year. Small of stature, blond, blue-eyed and of a cheerful disposition, Dolgushin was recognised as a natural pilot from the earliest days of the war.

He had a long and varied operational career, serving initially with the I-16-equipped 122.IAP at the time of the German invasion of the Soviet Union on 22 June 1941. Seeing action right from the start of Operation *Barbarossa*, Dolgushin transferred to 180.IAP on the West Front in August, having already scored a handful of kills. By February of 1942 he had flown 185 sorties and claimed 11 kills, and was made a Hero of the Soviet Union (HSU) three months later. In June of that year his regiment re-equipped with Hurricanes, and he claimed at least four kills with the British fighter prior to moving to the Yak-7B-equipped 434.IAP in August 1942. Soon renamed 32.Gu.IAP, this regiment saw extensive action on the Kalinin Front. Dolgushin, who had been promoted to kapitan and given command of an eskadrilya, scored a further six victories with 32.Gu.IAP.

He was given command of 156.IAP in October 1943 flying the La-5N, and then the La-7, Dolgushin remained in charge of the regiment right through to VE-Day. During his time in command, 156.IAP supported the liberation of Belorussia and Poland, before seeing action over northern Germany in the last months of the war. Dolgushin's final official victory tally stood at 17 individual and 11 shared kills, but to this should be added four individual claims denied him by his first regimental commissar (due to a clash of personalities!) in 1941. He remained in the air force until 1976.

LA-7 'WHITE 93' OF LT COL SERGEI DOLGUSHIN, COMMANDER OF 156.IAP, 215.IAD, 8.IAK, GERMANY, EARLY 1945

Sergei Dolgushin's distinctively marked La-7 had its upper surfaces painted in medium grey overall and the undersurfaces standard light blue. The nose was red as far as the second aluminium cowling band, and the gold star and red ribbon of the HSU were painted on the left side of the cowling. The red nose was adopted as a Corps air marking in September 1944 in response to an order issued by the commander of 8.IAK. Beneath the cockpit on the port side were four rows of victory stars, with the 17 in red denoting individual kills and the 11 in white shared victories. At the top of the fin was a small yellow Cyrillic letter in the shape of a reversed capital E, which signified 156.IAP's honorific designation 'Elbinskii', or Elbe, while to the right of it was the La-7's white factory marking.

AIRCRAFT SPECIFICATION
Lavochkin La-7

TYPE:	single-engined monoplane fighter
ACCOMMODATION:	pilot
DIMENSIONS:	length 29 ft 2.5 in (8.90 m) wingspan 32 ft 1.75 in (9.80 m) height 8 ft 6.25 in (2.60 m)
WEIGHTS:	empty 5842 lb (2620 kg) maximum take-off 7496 lb (3400 kg)
PERFORMANCE:	maximum speed 423 mph (680 kmh) range 615 miles (990 km) powerplant Shvetsov M-82FN output 1850 hp (1380 kW)
ARMAMENT:	two or three 20 mm cannon in upper cowling; provision for bombs or rockets under wings
FIRST FLIGHT DATE:	March 1942 (La-5)
OPERATOR:	Czechoslovakia, USSR
PRODUCTION:	9920 La-5s and 5753 La-7s

The first Lavochkin-designed fighter to see series production was the LaGG-3, which despite being one of the most modern fighters in the Soviet arsenal in June 1941, was not a match for the Luftwaffe fighters of the day. Underpowered and less manoeuvrable than the Bf 109F/G or Fw 190A, hundreds of LaGG-3s fell to the Jagdwaffe. Stunned by reports of the fighter's combat inadequacies, Lavochkin swiftly replaced the aircraft's inline M-105PF engine with the far more powerful Shvetsov M-82 radial in early 1942. The resulting fighter proved to be not only faster than its predecessor, but also more capable at medium to high altitudes. Designated the La-5, the first examples to reach the frontline (during the battle for Stalingrad in late 1942) were actually re-engined LaGG-3s. By late March 1943 production of the definitive La-5N had commenced, this variant featuring a fuel-injected M-82FN for better performance at altitude and cut down rear fuselage decking and a new canopy for better all-round vision. The La-5FN was more than a match for the Bf 109G, and could hold its own with the Fw 190. In November 1943 the further improved La-7 started flight trials, this model boasting even greater performance thanks to the lightening of its overall structure and adoption of the metal wing spars featured in late-build La-5FNs. Attention was also paid to reducing the fighter's drag coefficient, which resulted in the adoption of a revised cowling and inboard wing leading edge surfaces. The La-7 entered service in the spring of 1944, and went on to become the favoured mount of many Soviet aces. ∎

JAMES JABARA

James Jabara was born in Muskogee, Oklahoma, on 10 October 1923. His interest in aviation dated back to his formative years, when barnstorming was in its prime, but only 5ft 5in in height, and with poor eyesight, Jabara's dream of becoming a fighter pilot seemed almost impossible. Rumor has it that he consumed heavy doses of Vitamin A to improve his sight, and this apparently worked well enough for him to be accepted into the USAAF's pilot training programme right out of high school. He received his wings on 1 October 1943 and was posted to the Ninth Air Force's 382nd FS/363rd FG in England in April 1944.

Flying P-51B/Ds with the group, he claimed 1.5 aerial kills prior to returning home tour-expired in August. Jabara returned to England in February 1945 when he was posted to the 354th FS/355th FG, and he remained with the unit until war's end – by which time he had flown more than 100 missions. Staying in the air force post-war, Jabara attended Tactical Air School at Tyndall air force base and then completed a tour in Okinawa with the 53rd FG. He transitioned to the F-86A in 1950 and was posted to the 334th FIS/4th FIG. Jabara went to Korea with the unit in December 1950, and on 20 May 1951, he downed his fifth and sixth MiG-15s to become the first American jet ace. Jabara was immediately withdrawn from Korea and flown to Japan the very next day, senior USAF officers deeming the first jet ace too valuable to risk in combat.

Finally managing to get reassigned to the 4th FIG in January 1953, Jabara once again made an impact in the skies over Korea. By this stage of the war close to 800 MiG-15s were based north of the Yalu in Manchuria, so the hunting was much better than it had been in early 1951. By the time Jabara's second tour came to an end, he had 15 confirmed kills. This made him the second-highest scoring Sabre pilot of the Korean War. By 1966 Jabara was the youngest full colonel in the USAF at just 43 years of age. But he and his daughter were tragically killed in a car accident on 17 November 1966.

F-86A-5 SABRE 48-259 OF CAPT JAMES JABARA, 334TH FIS/4TH FIG, SUWON, MAY 1951

Seen in early 4th FIG colors, this machine was one of a string of Sabres used by James Jabara during his first tour in Korea, which lasted from December 1950 through to 20 May 1951. One of the oldest F-86s to see combat in the war, this aircraft was actually Jabara's assigned jet, although it appears that he never actually scored a kill while flying it. Transferred to the 336th FIS following its pilot's hasty departure home, 48-259 was lost on 9 November 1951 but the pilot survived.

AIRCRAFT SPECIFICATION
North American F-86 Sabre

TYPE:	jet fighter-bomber
ACCOMMODATION:	one pilot
DIMENSIONS:	(for F-86F) length 37 ft 6 in (11.43 m) wingspan 39 ft 1 in (11.9 m) height 14 ft 8.75 in (4.47 m)
WEIGHTS:	empty 11,125 lb (5045 kg) maximum take-off 20,611 lb (9350 kg)
PERFORMANCE:	maximum speed 678 mph (1091 kmh) range 850 miles (1368 km) with external tanks powerplant General Electric J47-GE-27 (F-86F) output 5970 lb st (26.56 kN)
ARMAMENT:	six Colt-Browning 0.5-in machine guns in forward fuselage sides
FIRST FLIGHT DATE:	27 November 1946
OPERATOR:	USA, UK, RAAF, SAAF, Japan, Norway, Pakistan, South Korea, Spain, West Germany, Canada
PRODUCTION:	9502

Aside from the Bell UH-1 Huey, no other post-war Western combat aircraft has been built in as great a numbers as the F-86. Total production amounted to 9502 airframes, covering no less than 13 separate land- and sea-based variants. The first contracts for the fighter were placed jointly by the USAAF and the US Navy in 1944, although the initial design featured unswept wings and a fuselage of greater diameter to allow it to house the Allison J35-2 engine. Following examination of captured German jet aircraft and related documentation, North American radically altered the design's shape. The revised XP-86 was a vastly superior machine, setting a new world speed record in 1949 thanks to the aerodynamic overhaul of its fuselage and incorporation of the all new GE J47 turbojet. F-86A Sabres were thrust into battle over Korea in December 1950, where the aircraft soon achieved the status of 'ace maker' in pitched battles against the MiG-15. Combat ushered in further improvements to the aircraft, while the radar-equipped F-86D also enjoyed widespread use with Air Defense Command as its first all-weather interceptor. A dynasty of Navy fighters in the form of the FJ-2/3 and -4 also served the fleet well into the late 1950s. Examples of the F-86 remained in the active inventory of a number of air forces into the early 1990s. ∎

I saw the armor-piercing incendiaries hit his fuselage and left wing. He did two violent snap rolls and started to spin. At 10,000 ft, with my wingman and I circling him, the MiG pilot bailed out.
– James Jabara

AVIHU BEN-NUN

Born in 1939, Avihu Ben-Nun joined the IDF at the age of 18 as required by Israeli Compulsory Military Service Law. He volunteered for the Israel Defense Forces/Air Force (IDF/AF) Flying School and duly trained as a fighter pilot, graduating in Class 29 on 19 November 1959. Having completed the fast jet conversion course at the Ouragan operational training unit, Ben-Nun then saw squadron service with the Mystere. He continued to fly the French fighter as a frontline Emergency Pilot (EP) during his subsequent reassignment to the Flying School as an instructor. In 1964 he returned to squadron service, flying the Shahak (Mirage III) with No 119 Sqn.

Shortly after the June 1967 Six Day War – during which Ben-Nun was the Senior Deputy Commander of Mystere-equipped No 116 Sqn – he was transferred to No 119 Sqn as Senior Deputy Commander. He marked his return to Shahaks with two Egyptian MiG-21 kills on 8 July and 10 October 1967. In 1969 Ben-Nun was selected to form No 69 Sqn, which was the IDF/AF's second Kurnass (Phantom II) unit. He led the squadron until 1972, and was credited with his third kill (a Soviet MiG-21) on 30 July 1970. Becoming a staff officer following his departure from No 69 Sqn, Ben-Nun still saw regular combat in the unit's Kurnass as an EP. Indeed, he was credited with his fourth, and last, kill (a Syrian Su-7) on 9 September 1972, soon after leaving No 69 Sqn. Ben-Nun also flew eight missions during the October 1973 Yom Kippur War.

A leader from birth, Ben-Nun was promoted to full colonel in 1975 as head of the IDF/AF's Operations Department, and then served as Hatzor air base commander between 1977 and 1979. Promoted to brigadier general, Ben-Nun duly commanded Tel-Nof air base until 1982, when he became head of the Air Group and then IDF/AF Chief of Staff. Ben-Nun's assignment to the IDF Staff as Head of Planning, with the rank of major general, between June 1985 and July 1987 proved to be the stepping-stone which led to him being made IDF/AF commander between 22 September 1987 and 2 January 1992, when Ben-Nun finally retired. By then he had flown some 5000 hours, mostly in combat aircraft, and completed 450 operational sorties, during which he had claimed four kills.

KURNASS 183 OF NO 69 SQN, RAMAT DAVID, 9 SEPTEMBER 1972

The first Kurnass Su-7 kill was achieved by No 69 Sqn's former CO Avihu Ben-Nun (and his navigator Zvi Kesler), who was by then flying with the unit as an emergency posting pilot, in Kurnass 183. Ben-Nun was credited with four kills, two of which were scored in the Mirage III in 1967 and the remaining pair as a Kurnass pilot in 1970 and 1972.

AIRCRAFT SPECIFICATION
McDonnell Douglas F-4 Phantom II
(all dimensions and performance data for the F-4E)

TYPE:	all-weather jet interceptor
ACCOMMODATION:	two-man crew seated in tandem
DIMENSIONS:	length 63 ft 0 in (19.20 m) wingspan 38 ft 4 in (11.68 m) height 16 ft 5 in (5.05 m)
WEIGHTS:	empty 30,328 lb (13,757 kg) maximum take-off 61,795 lb (28,030 kg)
PERFORMANCE:	maximum speed 1434 mph (2307 kmh) range 1613 miles (2596 km) ferry range powerplant two General Electric J79-GE-17 turbojets output 35,800 lb st (165 kN)
ARMAMENT:	one General Electric M61A1 20 mm rotary cannon in the nose; four AIM-7E-2 Sparrow missiles (intercept mission configuration) in underfuselage troughs; up to 16,000-lb (7258 kg) of external ordnance in various combinations
FIRST FLIGHT DATE:	27 May 1958
OPERATOR:	USA, UK, RAAF, Japan, Germany, South Korea, Spain, Egypt, Israel, Turkey, Greece, Iran
PRODUCTION:	5211

The most famous post-World War 2 fighter, the F-4 Phantom II is still very much a part of today's military scene, with examples being flown by nine air forces across the globe. However, this number is shrinking by the year, with most of the 5211 built during a 19-year production run having now been retired. Initially developed as a company private venture by McDonnell, the Phantom II evolved from an attack aircraft armed with four 20 mm cannon to an advanced, gunless, all-weather interceptor, boasting state-of-the-art radar and advanced missiles. Ordered by the US Navy for deployment aboard its carriers, the first production F-4Bs were delivered in December 1960. The following year a fly-off took place between a Navy Phantom II and various frontline USAF fighter types, with the results clearly showing that the F-4 was vastly superior to its Air Force contemporaries. The USAF immediately ordered the aircraft, and the jet went on to equip 16 of its 23 fighter wings within Tactical Air Command. The advent of the Vietnam War thrust the Phantom II into action, and the design's true multi-role capability soon saw it delivering tons of bombs in large-scale attack formations. Improved versions of the Phantom II (F-4E and F-4J) also made their debut in combat in the late 1960s. ■

RA'ANAN YOSEF

Born in 1949, Ra'anan Yosef joined the IDF at 18 as required by Israeli Compulsory Military Service Law. He volunteered for the IDF/AF Flying School (FS), where he trained as a fighter pilot. Yosef undertook his training shortly after the Six Day War, when the fighter course was seen to be the most prestigious military assignment in Israel. He graduated with Class 62 on 16 July 1970, less than a month before the Attrition War came to an end.

Assigned to No 113 Sqn's fighter pilots' Operational Training Unit (OTU) Course, Yosef trained on the Ouragan from August through to November 1970. He was then assigned to No 105 Sqn, where he flew both Super Mystere B 2s (SMB 2) and the locally-upgraded Sa'ar – an SMB 2 re-engined with a Pratt & Whitney J52 turbojet.

In early 1971 Yosef began his conversion onto the Shahak (Mirage III), having had just eight months of fast jet experience – four months in an Ouragan OTU and four months flying the SMB 2 and Sa'ar. Piloting the IDF/AF's premier interceptor with No 101 Sqn, Yosef was a regular squadron pilot until December 1972, when he was assigned to the Flying School to complete an Instructor's Course. His squadron status then changed, as he went from being a regular pilot to an Emergency Posting (EP) pilot, flying the Shahak one day a week.

With tension rising just prior to the outbreak of the October 1973 Yom Kippur War, the EP aircrews were ordered to join their squadrons on a full-time basis. Yosef flew just a single operational mission with No 101 Sqn before being transferred to No 113 Sqn, which was short of experienced fighter pilots following its recent transition onto the Nesher. Yosef completed an astounding 41 operational missions between 6 and 24 October, as well as two ferry flights and a single test flight! Flying as a wingman throughout the war, Yosef participated in five aerial combats and was credited with three confirmed kills.

Retiring from the IDF/AF in 1975 after completing his five years' service commitment, Yosef subsequently flew the Nesher and then the Kfir as a reserve pilot until 1985.

I opened fire and hit the empennage. The MiG lost control, its braking 'chute was deployed, and when it was nearly vertical, pointing downwards, the pilot ejected.
– Ra'anan Yosef

NESHER 61 OF GIORA EPSTEIN, NO 113 SQN, HATZOR AIR BASE, 20 OCTOBER 1973

Although a No 101 Sqn pilot, Epstein downed eight aircraft while flying No 113 Sqn's Nesher 61. This aircraft was also flown by Ra'anan Yosef on five combat missions between 9 and 23 October 1973, although unlike Epstein, he did not claim any victories with it.

AIRCRAFT SPECIFICATION

IAI Nesher

TYPE:	jet fighter-bomber
ACCOMMODATION:	one pilot
DIMENSIONS:	length 51 ft 0.5 in (15.56 m) wingspan 26 ft 11.5 in (8.22 m) height 13 ft 11.5 in (4,25 m)
WEIGHTS:	eempty 15,763 lb (7150 kg) maximum take-off 30,200 lb (13,700 kg)
PERFORMANCE:	maximum speed 1451 mph (2335 kmh) range 777 miles (1250 km) with external tanks powerplant IAI Bedek Aviation Division-built SNECMA Atar 09C output 13,670 lb st (61 kN)
ARMAMENT:	Two DEFA 30 mm cannon in underfuselage; two Rafael Shafrir or AIM-9 Sidewinder missiles; provision for up to 4000-lb (1814 kg) of external ordnance in various combinations
FIRST FLIGHT DATE:	21 March 1971
OPERATOR:	Israel, Argentina
PRODUCTION:	61

Effectively a Mirage 5 built by Israeli Aircraft Industries without the benefit of a manufacturing licence, the Nesher differed from the Dassault product only in having a Martin-Baker JM 6 zero-zero ejection seat, some Israeli-developed avionics and internal wiring that allowed the aircraft to carry either the home-grown Rafael Shafrir or the AIM-9 Sidewinder. The first of 61 Neshers was handed over to the IDF/AF in 1971. Initial deliveries augmented the strength of the Mirage III-equipped Nos 101 and 117 Sqns, but the side-by-side operation of the two types resulted in unfair comparisons being made. The Nesher was heavier, with a higher fuel fraction, so no mixed formations were flown as it was thought that the Mirage III pilots would have to disengage from combat before the Neshers. The Nesher was also a better fighter-bomber, and in a mixed formation on an air-to-ground mission, the Mirage III's presence would be a handicap. Surprisingly, Nesher pilots were unable to exploit all their advantages against the older Mirage IIIs in dissimilar air combat training, where agility and manoeuvrability counted. Such training sessions ended when one of the participants reached bingo fuel. Frustrated pilots immediately preferred the Mirage III, but in combat the differences between the Nesher and the original delta fighter did not seem that significant, although the Nesher's better combat endurance was of great importance. Replaced in frontline service by the Kfir, most surviving Neshers were refurbished by IAI and sold to Argentina as Daggers between 1978 and 1982. ■